D1266874

LADY JANE GREY

Lady Jane Grey
The portrait attributed to Master John

LADY JANE GREY

The Setting of the Reign

DAVID MATHEW

EYRE METHUEN
LONDON

First published 1972
© 1972 David Mathew
Printed in Great Britain for
Eyre Methuen Ltd, 11 New Fetter Lane
London EC4P 4EE by
The Bowering Press, Plymouth

413 27980 4

FOR
JEANNE LADY CAMOYS

Contents

Illustrations   *page* 9
Preface   11

Part One . *Lord Lisle*

I   Empson and Dudley   19
II   Kingston Lisle   23
III   King Henry's Court   27
IV   The Pale of Calais   30
V   The Lord Admiral   36
VI   The King's Will   41
VII   The New Reign   48

Part Two . *The Conflict*

I   The Rising in the West   54
II   The Norfolk Rising   61
III   Lord Seymour's End   69
IV   The Young King   76
V   Somerset's Fall   80
VI   Northumberland's Power   85

Part Three . *Northumberland*

I   The Rise of Cecil   89
II   The Old Religion   92
III   Emerging Forces   99
IV   The Continental Scene   101
V   The Explorations   106
VI   The Palatinate of Durham   113
VII   The Religious Background   118
VIII   The Secretary of State   122

Part Four · Lady Jane Grey

I	The Succession	*page* 126
II	Lady Jane Grey	130
III	The King's Last Days	135
IV	The Tower: A Palace	142
V	The Northern Progress	148
VI	The Tower: A Prison	152
VII	Queen Mary's Judgment	155
VIII	Epilogue	159

Appendices

The Portraiture of Northumberland	167
Select Chart Pedigrees	169
Select Bibliography	181
Index	183

Illustrations

Frontispiece Lady Jane Grey   *(National Portrait Gallery)*

between pages 80 and 81

1   Edward IV   *(National Portrait Gallery)*
2   The Duke of Somerset   *(The Marquess of Bath)*
3   William Paget   *(National Portrait Gallery)*

between pages 96 and 97

4   The Duke of Northumberland   *(Mary Evans Picture Gallery)*
5   Thomas Cranmer   *(National Portrait Gallery)*
6   Bradgate Park   *(Bodleian Library, Oxford)*

Preface

This new study entitled *Lady Jane Grey* is in effect a sequel to *The Courtiers of Henry VIII*, for the two sovereigns who both died as minors, Edward VI and Lady Jane Grey, were wholly dominated by two of King Henry's courtiers, the Dukes of Somerset and Northumberland. King Henry was a powerful sovereign and the over-spill of his reign can be traced for several years. The book's sub-title is *The Setting of the Reign*, that brief period of the nine-days reign of Lady Jane in 1553.

Two factors cover this short time, the rule and ideas of King Edward VI, whose determination to maintain the Protestant religion resulted in the 'devise' of the Crown to Lady Jane; and the notions of the Duke of Northumberland, who was wholly responsible for the carrying out of that reign's policy.

In spite of a certain passivity, the consequence of her youthfulness and her sex, Lady Jane Grey is the key figure of all this period. She is always presented as a royal person, the elaborate costume, the ropes of pearls. She was a strange figure in an English setting, a true Renaissance princess. Her Calvinism can only be understood after considering the foreign influences which played upon her. It is one of the side consequences that could she have been successful there would probably have been a unity between the effects of the Reformation in England and in Scotland. It is important to distinguish her parents' *rôle* and especially the character of her mother the Duchess of Suffolk. Throughout the earlier portions of this book Lady Jane is very gradually brought forward towards the centre of the scene.

Except for a few months the whole of her brief life was passed at her parents' remote house in the great park at Bradgate in Leicestershire with its woods and lakes, below the limestone ridges of Charnwood Forest. She was brought up in the Renaissance tradition of Marguerite, Queen of Navarre, the sister of Francis I, and to this was added the new religious doctrine. It seems that she was envisaged by those who approached her from abroad as the

destined bride of Edward VI and this explains her correspondence
with the Swiss Reformer Bullinger. She was addressed as a patron
and protectress, a future sovereign. There is very little correspondence with her contemporaries; I think that it is difficult to
exaggerate her loneliness.

Lady Jane Grey was the heir-general of her mother, the Duchess
of Suffolk, who was herself the elder daughter and co-heiress of
Henry VIII's sister, Mary Queen of France, by her second husband,
Charles Brandon. The old King had always looked after his
cousins the Dorset family, but he had no warmth towards his
cousin the young Marquess, who later became the Duke of Suffolk.
There were two younger sisters; but Lady Jane had no other close
relations. Her tutor, John Aylmer, with whom she studied Plato,
was a young man and a *protégé* of her father's. He would later
develop along very different lines. Under Queen Elizabeth he was
Bishop of London and a forerunner of the Laudians.

From all these circumstances Lady Jane had a very slender
experience of life on which was grafted a burning religious faith.
In this and in this alone she bore a resemblance to the almost contemporary leader of the French Huguenots, Jeanne d'Albret, the
Queen of Navarre. Although she was so very young, it was impossible to mould her. To this secluded life and passionate doctrine
there could hardly be a greater contrast than the easy-going ways
of thought of the Duke of Northumberland.

As soon as the 'devise' had been completed, excluding from the
succession to the Throne both the young King's step-sisters, the
Lady Mary and the Lady Elizabeth, the Duke must have dealt
with Lady Jane Grey's parents. The Duke of Suffolk was a nonentity and never much interested in his daughter; the motive
power resided in the young girl's mother. As she grew middle-
aged, the Duchess with her broad face and her heavy shoulders
came to resemble her uncle Henry VIII. It is interesting to trace
the moves she made.

Sir John Dudley, who later became the Duke of Northumberland, was before all else a soldier. He was in some respects an old-
fashioned statesman, tied to the accumulation of landed wealth
which he would obtain from the great sequestrated lands of the
see of Durham. He was bound to the idea of the old families,

claiming to be the co-heir to the Beauchamps, Earls of Warwick. He was also through his mother's family, the Greys, Lords Lisle, a distant cousin of the Lady Jane's. Since his childhood he had been an Henrican courtier.

John Dudley was the eldest surviving son of Henry VII's minister, Edmund Dudley. An account is given in Part One of the Lisle peerage, which he eventually inherited; this was based on Kingston Lisle among the beech trees under the wide, bald shoulder of the Berkshire downs. An account is also given in Part One of the rule of Dudley's step-father Lord Lisle in the Pale of Calais. We can observe this scene so closely on account of the mass of documentation which remains from this range of years, and can view the Court from a little distance.

At the beginning of the reign of Edward VI (1547) we can discern four principal figures. There had been no room for faction at Henry VIII's Court; that meant that the great officers were each a solitary as was their young sovereign. The laymen who would become the Dukes of Somerset and Northumberland, and also Archbishop Cranmer, all operated consciously in isolation. Further the future dukes were in each case leaders of very limited political abilities. There was no man in that period who had the skill with which Cardinal Wolsey or Thomas Cromwell had exercised their power in politics. The two dukes in their different ways had little foresight.

When Henry VIII died, John Dudley, now Lord Lisle, passed inevitably into rivalry with Seymour, who became the Protector Somerset. At this stage he was always helped by his own decisive character and a favouring tide. His happy years ended in 1552 when he killed the Duke of Somerset.

Something of magnanimity vanished from the reign when Somerset suffered execution. From that day Northumberland went alone down the short grim years that still remained to him. To my mind the Duke of Somerset is the most interesting of these four characters. He was in some ways like a great flawed diamond. He was an ardent but not an intemperate devotee of the reformed religion. This gave him a sympathy with all men, for the most part citizens of London and the East Country towns, who shared his judgments. There is no doubt that this offended the men of his own high class. It was this link also which led some of the Duke's ideas to be Utopian. On the other hand his character was seamed by greed. He could not resist the fact that lands could come to him so very easily. He was the only one of his generation to suffer from ideas of architectural grandeur, as can be seen in Somerset House and in the country palace that he planned in Savernake Forest in Wiltshire. It seems to me that at least in the field of politics he was wholly without imagination. These were years in which a more perspicacious man could have seen John Dudley as his future rival. He did not realize this danger until it was almost upon him. In all his processes he was very solitary.

Edward VI was a cold-hearted boy. He always kept his reverence for his great father. He lost him early and his life was starved of affection; in any case his nature was not affectionate. Compared to other youths in the sixteenth century we know a great deal about him. He was not so learned or so full of knowledge as he was taught to think himself. His relationship with his two successive governors was difficult. He was very conscious of his royal blood; he did not value his uncle and cousins on the distaff side. His contact with his uncle Somerset grew very cold. I think that he resented any man's attempt to *manage* him. As to Northumberland, the King was an intelligent little boy and I believe that in this case his relationship was a compound of respect well-mixed with fear.

He seems to have had no serious relations with the many sons of the great lords who were his contemporaries and were kept about him. In any case there is no evidence that they shared in his precocious interest in his religion. Like others of his station whose sexual development was slow, it was easy for him to see himself as a Holy King. He enjoyed sitting in his high seat, while his divines preached at him. These tastes would separate him from other children and youths of high position. He had a single friend of no political significance, Barnaby Fitzpatrick, a boy, Irish and Protestant, who later became Lord Upper Ossory.

During the later years of his short life King Edward thought that he would marry the Princess of France, to whom he was betrothed, the beautiful Elisabeth de Valois. She was in his judgment his only equal and he had a curious hope in the help, even the guidance that he might receive from Henry II of France. The fact that he and his future bride were of different religions never seems to have been mentioned. King Edward was convinced that he would bring to his people the milk of the Gospel and the Truth of God's Word. It seems that as he lay dying it was blindingly evident to him that of all his family it was only his cousin Lady Jane who was a true-hearted Protestant. He bequeathed to her a kingdom which, as far as its official religious dispositions were concerned, she had no desire to alter. Some account of his reign is necessary to understand the rule of the nine-days Queen; for this was a continuation of Edwardian values.

The fourth principal character is Thomas Cranmer the Archbishop of Canterbury, who plays a curiously muted part in the political happenings of all this period. He had been much cosseted by Henry VIII and he now found himself faced by two successive governors who each in his different way was more intractable. And then Dr Cranmer's views were changing and his foreign contacts were always broadening. He was strangely enough in a true sense an ecclesiastic. It was part of his charm that there was no churchman in England who was very far from him. Among the Bishops of the conservative opposition, both Veysey and Tunstall were among his friends. Of course there was one thing which linked the prelates of this reign all together; they had none of them refused the Royal Supremacy.

The question of Archbishop Cranmer's relations with the Duke of Somerset is rather difficult for when the crisis came he did not support him. It is likely that on the one hand the Duke's love of money and the grandeur of his building plans put him out of touch with the Archbishop's modest scale of life at Lambeth and, on the other hand, Somerset's Utopian notions would have found no echo. At the same time it must be said that perhaps the Archbishop was too mild for the harsh realities of the sixteenth-century English politics.

Certainly his relations with Northumberland were never good. All that could be said was that the new leader was by definition a supporter of the Established Church. That position he would retain as long as he was in power, for the dioceses, and he had in mind Durham, had great lands which he was determined to gain for his own use. But this period also included the time of Dr

Cranmer's closest association with the Protestants upon the Continent.

By this time Lady Jane Grey had moved towards the centre of the picture. Her parents' wealth had increased by inheritance from the dead young Dukes of Suffolk; they gained, too, from Somerset's destruction. Northumberland's mind was bent upon the great commercial benefits of exploration, a subject which had left Somerset quite cold. This was something which needed no foreign help and could be brought about by English ships and English money. Moreover this was a line of action which needed a dictator and not a cabinet; it chimed well with Northumberland's own mood. But the greater part of his time was occupied by his new plans for the succession.

His isolation served to mar his judgment. He could not see how his project for the Crown would be received by his great equals. Of course in the choice of Lady Jane the King's own fervent character had played its part. The Duke had determined to win to his side certain elements among the richer houses. Suffolk was like putty in his hands. He arranged the betrothal of Lady Jane's child sister to the son of Lord Grey de Wilton. His own unmarried daughter and Lady Jane's next sister were married to the Earls of Huntingdon and Pembroke. Lady Jane herself was married to Lord Guildford Dudley, his own eldest unmarried son.

Lady Jane Grey was at her father's house at Sheen when King Edward died. She was a small princess, slender with long tapering fingers and red-gold lights in her hair. She was taken to the palace in the Tower of London; her cousin King Edward had stayed there while waiting for his own coronation. She went downstream in lovely weather on a warm day in July. Her relations with her young husband were not easy. The boy and girl had been brought up in very different moral climates. She was quite tart with his desire to share the crown matrimonial with her.

She was now surrounded by the Duke and Duchess of Northumberland and the Duke and Duchess of Suffolk, her own parents, the Archbishop of Canterbury, a somewhat equivocal figure, and by many of the chief peers of the kingdom, the Duke's new friend the Earl of Pembroke, and the Marquess of Winchester. In very truth all, except the Duke, were lords in waiting. The Lady Mary,

Edward's sister, was still in England and at liberty and was gathering support. There was no way by which Queen Jane could secure the lords' fidelity. Day after day her situation was beginning to fall to pieces. She was in the purest sense a victim of power politics. When it was all over, she and the Duke were both beheaded. He returned to the old faith and she died in the new religion. I have carefully amassed such information as we can now obtain. It is one of those cases in which the reader's own views are bound to count in an assessment of the situation.

In all my books and especially in this I have benefited from the constant help and guidance of my brother Gervase. I am grateful to Dr A. L. Rowse for his comments on Southampton's religious outlook and for his help in regard to aspects of Northumberland's private interests; and to Dr Claire Cross for information as to Lady Huntingdon.

DAVID MATHEW

Stonor Park
April 1972

B

I

Empson and Dudley

Edmund Dudley was the chief financial agent of Henry VII, one of the wise Kings of late fifteenth-century Europe. He was without friends and aroused by his exactions a host of enemies. These persuaded the young Henry VIII to put him to death. Thus the main features of his life are familiar to us; but little else is known about him or about his colleague, Sir Richard Empson, who was his partner as financial agent and worked and died with him. Henry VII was a secret King and did not reveal the methods by which he chose private men to raise his funds for him.

The Wars of the Roses had just ended and it was important for Henry VII to avoid all personal responsibility for paring the wealth of those who had in many cases been his chief supporters. It thus fell to Empson and Dudley to compel the great landowners to enter into recognizances to keep the peace and to collect the feudal dues and other taxes from them. It was asserted that both men went beyond their legal powers and that pardons for outlawry were purchased. The real difficulty lay in the fact that so long as Henry VII lived there was no means of appeal against their judgments.

There is a reflection here of the policy and line of action of Louis XI. Both sovereigns had a calm and calculated judgment that they should take what steps they could to check the growing power of their wealthy subjects. It was also evident that the ministers of such a policy would be destroyed upon their masters' death.

It is characteristic of the feelings of that time that both these royal servants should have been described as men of humble birth,

Dudley as the grandson of a carpenter in Staffordshire, and Empson as the son of a sievemaker in Towcester. Both these assertions are now known to be false. It seems likely that Empson first attracted Henry VII's attention and then brought forward the young Edmund Dudley. They were both members of Parliament and each in turn was speaker of the House of Commons. Dudley was born about 1462 and was from an early date in the King's reign a privy councillor. To us this sounds a great promotion; but it may be explained by Sidney Lee's suggestion that in their judicial capacity Empson and Dudley acted as a sub-committee of the privy council.

They were both in fact by origin of a certain substance. Empson had a fortune as well as lands in the neighbourhood of Towcester and Dudley had inherited in 1500 manors in the Rape of Bramber from his father, who had been sheriff of Sussex. They were both, however, isolated men living side by side in houses in St Swithin's Lane within the City. Dudley was under-sheriff of London. He was a member of Gray's Inn and at the time of his death he had acquired much landed property. This was in addition to Bramshott in Hampshire and the three manors of Catcombe, Calbourne and Whitwell in the Isle of Wight, which had come to him by inheritance. A detailed account has survived of his large town house and of its contents. There was a great hall with two galleries facing out upon a garden. The furnishing was good, but not elaborate. The front hall had a tapestry behind the dais. The great parlour had hangings of red and green buckram and curtains of green say. The little parlour was provided with curtains of green say and beyond this lay the counting house. The long gallery had curtains of blue and yellow buckram, a carpet and a French chair. In the square chamber there was a bed covered with white fustian fringed with gilt wooden balls. There were curtains of white linen to surround the bed, a feather mattress and a bolster and five pillows and a tapestry counterpane. The gallery beside the great chamber had green and red buckram hangings with green curtains at the windows and a coffer with piles of bills. The great chamber itself had another feather bed with an embroidered tester and a coffer with Edmund Dudley's garments. There was a closet which contained 1650 ounces of silver plate. The impression here conveyed is of a house that, even for its period, had not much luxury. But it was clearly the residence of a man of substance.

It seems that men had realized that it was necessary for Henry VIII's reign to start without the difficulty that must have been created if lawyers, who had built up his father's fortune for him, were left at liberty. Empson and Dudley were both placed in the Tower. During his time in prison Edmund Dudley composed his only surviving work, *The Tree of Commonwealth*, a treatise in favour of absolute monarchy. This was written under strain and one would not expect lightheartedness or wit; but in truth it is didactic and so dull as to be almost unreadable. There was at present much to worry him. One can only say that as far as we can now trace, it is difficult to see in Edmund Dudley any resemblance to his famous son.

Empson and Dudley were kept in the Tower of London for eighteen months. It seems that the new King or his immediate advisers were reluctant to proceed with their execution; but the hatred raised against them in the House of Commons was in the end too strong to allow of their reprieve. The area of support for Edmund Dudley is revealed by his will that was signed the day before his execution. Thus his son Jerome, presumably at that time his heir, was placed under four guardians. This was an impressive list and included Bishop FitzJames of London, Dean Colet of St Paul's and Sir Andrew Windsor, who was his first wife's brother. With the exception of the layman, these guardians were not men of the Court. The actual charge made against both Empson and Dudley was that of summoning their friends to attend them under arms in the event of the King's death. In his will he expressed a desire, which was not carried out, that he should be buried in Westminster Abbey. It seems that he did not understand that he was to be sacrificed. His son Jerome did not long survive him. Little more is known of Edmund Dudley.

In spite of his isolation he had certain relationships which would fructify in his son's lifetime. In the male line he was himself a cousin of a house of obscure peers, the Lords Dudley, whose possessions then included Dudley Castle in the centre of what was later to become the Black Country in the Midlands. He had made two marriages, the first when he was a young man, with a widow, Mrs Corbet, who had four young children. She died leaving Dudley an only daughter. When he was a widower he married Elizabeth Grey with whose family he had certain dealings.[1] She was the youngest daughter of Lord Lisle and on her father's death he had become her guardian and her marriage had been granted to him. She was at that time in no sense an heiress. By her he left three sons. The second, John, was, in time, to be the Duke of Northumberland.

[1] At his death in 1492 Lord Lisle had held the manor of Kingston Lisle from Edmund Dudley, *The Complete Peerage*, vol. viii, p. 60.

II

Kingston Lisle

The manor of Kingston Lisle lies on a shoulder of the downs in the western part of Berkshire, where fields slip down into the Vale of the White Horse. The chief house in the parish was Sparsholt, which has not survived. The bare land, which carried sheep, lay above the beech trees in the rich valley. It was as distances were considered in the fifteenth century not remote; only some thirty miles to the eastwards there lay those royal forests which formed the hunting lands round Windsor Castle.

Kingston had been the centre of the Lisle inheritance, brought, on the extinction of that family, to the great Earl of Shrewsbury with his second wife. The son of this bed, John Lord Lisle, was killed beside his aged father, the famous soldier, in a small fight at Chatillon in Périgord, when the English at last were being driven from their long hold in Aquitaine. The title passed first to his son and then to his daughter.

The next generations formed the background which young John Dudley constantly recalled as he climbed to power. For a relatively brief period, about a century and a half, it had become the practice of the Crown to call to the House of Lords the husbands who were guardians, in right of their wives, of noble lands. These peerages *jure uxoris* were peculiar to England. They were not found in Scotland, nor on the continent save in Castile; but there the husband took all his wife's titles and men were also entitled to divert their descent to younger children. In England it was only the lowest rank of the peerage, the baronies, which were thus affected. It was useful for certain of the great families to have seats for their cadets in the House of Lords.

Thus in 1474 Sir Edward Grey, the young brother-in-law of

Queen Elizabeth, the wife of Edward IV, was created Lord Lisle
on his marriage to the Talbot heiress. His own properties were in
the Midlands and he was granted Astley and other manors in
Leicestershire and Warwickshire. He was also Constable of Kenilworth. These matters were important for John Dudley. It was not
only the Lisle title. Kenilworth, Warwick and Northumberland
would come before him as his dreams expanded. It is seldom
remembered that his mother belonged to the same family as Lady
Jane Grey, whom he was to champion.

The last male member of this branch of the family, John Lord
Lisle, had been born in 1480 and came into his inheritance as a
child of ten. His younger sister was married to Edmund Dudley.
He himself had married Lady Marcella (called also Muriel and
Myryell), one of the daughters of the second Duke of Norfolk, the
marriage taking place in those hard years before the dukedom was
restored after the victory of Flodden. He died at Sparsholt a few
months after his wedding and was taken across the vale to lie in his
tomb at the monastery of Abingdon. In the early spring of 1505
his widow gave birth to a posthumous daughter.

The history of this little girl, besides being a necessary prelude
to John Dudley's life, throws a flood of light upon the customs of
the time. When a few months old, she passed into the control of
her stepfather Sir Thomas Knyvett of Buckenham in Norfolk, who
was killed in a naval action against the French off Brest in August
1512. She was seven years of age and her mother was now dead.
Her marriage and wardship were then granted to Sir Charles
Brandon, a rising courtier, who was in need of some provision. In
1513 he was formally betrothed to his young ward and was created
Viscount Lisle with remainder to the children whom he should
have by her; but his fortunes were in the ascendant and two years
later he married Henry VIII's sister, Mary Queen of France. He
was created Duke of Suffolk and surrendered the patent of his
viscounty. The guardianship was then granted to the Countess of
Devon, the surviving daughter of Edward IV. The Courtenays
were unworldly in these matters and, though the girl had no great
portion to add to their very extensive properties, she was married
to the Countess's son, Henry Earl of Devon, who played a part
later in the reign as the Marquess of Exeter. Elizabeth, Countess

of Devon and Viscountess Lisle, died as a virgin bride in the late spring of 1519.

These details have their significance for they give us all that we can now know of someone who remained upon the periphery of history. They indicate the nature of the life of a young hereditary peeress of no great wealth whose wardship became of interest to the Crown since her marriage would bring her husband into the Upper House. On a rather lower social level the wardship would be granted within the ranks of the family or its close friendship. In Lady Lisle's case the wardship fell to strangers; this brought about a combination of respect and distant coldness. There was, too, a readiness on the part of the wife to give obedience.

The Lisle claim passed to John Dudley's mother, who had made a second marriage with Arthur Plantagenet. He was slightly his wife's junior and the King granted the pair two of Edmund Dudley's forfeited manors. In 1512 John Dudley was 'restored in blood'. This seems to imply that whatever his father's imprudences may have been, these were committed in the service of his royal master.

At the same time, John Dudley was placed under the guardianship of Sir Edward Guilford, Marshal of Calais. It may seem strange that his stepfather was not made his guardian but according to the practice of that time the ward was often married to his guardian's daughter. His stepfather was childless, nor was he in any sense a man of means. The Guilfords were a distinguished Court family settled at Rolvenden in Kent. All John Dudley's connections, and not only Arthur Plantagenet, were to benefit from the new King's reign. His elder stepsister, Elizabeth Dudley, was married to William Stourton, who became in time the seventh Lord Stourton, while her uncle, Sir Andrew, was created in 1529 Lord Windsor of Stanwell. These families, with the Guilfords, all belonged to the rather old-fashioned Court stocks, loyal and conservative.

It seems likely that John Dudley, as a youth, had all the qualities for success. He was frank and athletic and quite without book-learning. He always had great courage. His character seems to have been exactly what the young King liked to see. Dudley married his guardian's daughter Jane Guilford, who was an heiress, about the time that he came of age. They had a very numerous family, mainly sons. There is no evidence that he was other than a faithful husband. Meanwhile the Lisle inheritance had fallen in.

Although the Countess of Devon had died in 1519, it was not until four years later that Lady Plantagenet's husband received the Lisle peerage. By that time her elder sister, who had married Sir John Willoughby of Wollaton, had died childless. In 1523 her husband was created Viscount Lisle with remainder to the heirs male of his wife Elizabeth.

Lord Lisle, Sir Arthur Plantagenet, was in general fortunate, but one is always conscious that he would have risen faster and built up a much greater career had he been a son of Henry VII, instead of a bastard of the former dynasty. He was also very pious with a devotion to Our Lady of Walsingham; this was a quality which, in time, Henry VIII found wearing.

Lord Lisle's life may be said to have been concentrated on the defence of the English Channel, first in the Royal Navy and later as Governor of Calais. Until his last months, his life went smoothly; he continuously held his high appointments. The key point in his rise was his nomination in 1524 as a Knight of the Garter. He became Vice-Admiral of England in 1525, a post that he held until he went to Calais in 1533. Three years later he was made Warden of the Cinque Ports, so that henceforward he was the chief officer on both sides of the Narrow Seas. He always had an affection for, and a close relationship with, his youthful stepson. His first wife died, leaving no children by him, about 1530 and he married again in the next year. For many years there was this friendly influence behind John Dudley.

III

King Henry's Court

Viewed from Sir John Dudley's standpoint, for he received his knighthood in 1523, the reign of Henry VIII must have been a singularly happy time, a period of constantly burgeoning prosperity. He was never a favourite of any sovereign; but he showed himself a soldierly young man, who was always ready to defend his master's kingdom. It is not always remembered that for those who were far from the tide-rips of power, it was in many ways a happy Court. Throughout all the earlier years of his reign the King's goodwill beamed down upon his followers. The removal of the old-fashioned top hamper, like that associated with the Duke of Buckingham, could only have been encouraging to the younger generation. Friars and monks and monasteries meant nothing to young Dudley. Although he was caught up with it in later life, the world of prelacy was far away. No more than any other young soldier had he any interest in theology. The views of the Bishop of Rochester and Sir Thomas More meant nothing to him. He had all the outlook of a young Englishman of the upper classes about learning. Indeed of all that *galère* it seems quite likely that the only one whom he would understand was Lady More. Another way of putting this is to suggest that the only people whom he would understand were those who were ready to carry out their sovereign's bidding. However this may be, it certainly would seem that the changes of the King's reign passed him by.

He had never known any other sovereign. He had been a boy on the fringes of the Court when King Henry had been married to the Princess of Aragon. He must have had respect for her high position; but he never liked a Spaniard or indeed any other foreigner. In the time of Queen Catherine's successors he had been lucky. He had never come within the dangerous circle of their intimacy. With his wife's background in the Kentish squirearchy this might have been possible with Anne Boleyn; but his nature and interests were too military for the kind of young men who were her friends.

He had been eighteen at the Field of the Cloth of Gold (1520) and in a loose way one of the Duke of Suffolk's then dependents. The political moguls meant nothing to him; like all the English gentry, increasing as their scale of wealth diminished, he had a strong desire to mock the French. In 1532 he became joint Constable of Warwick Castle and two years later gained the post of Master of the Armoury of the Tower of London. He was to retain this office for ten years. He was a man who really knew the strength of England.

What were the meaning and the nature of Dudley's rise? Our knowledge of his early life is, as has been said, fragmentary, nor is it easy to understand the circumstances of his promotion. In the case of the King's two great ministers Cardinal Wolsey and Thomas Cromwell, it is not difficult to understand the nature of their rise. Curiously enough both were helped at an early stage of their careers by the same family, the King's cousins, the Marquesses of Dorset. For the rest Wolsey followed the well-worn steps of the political ecclesiastic. It was when he was Dean of Lincoln that his great talents revealed themselves to the new King. Thomas Cromwell rose through the Cardinal; he survived the gaudy wreck of that career and then placed his wide knowledge at the disposal of his anxious sovereign. He suffered more than any other minister of his period from being in essence a manipulator of his nation's finances.

In the case of the Duke of Somerset the parallel with Dudley is much closer for, in the first place, they were contemporaries. Somerset had energy and breadth of mind and a curious gentleness; but in the end he owed his whole position to being the elder brother of Henry VIII's third wife. It might be said that in a minor sense the Duke of Suffolk was Dudley's protector and he certainly obtained for him his early knighthood; but he was never the leader of a party, he was too lazy for that. With no other likely patrons yet appearing, it seems probable that the man who selected Dudley was the King. He had an eye for courage and it seems he had a confidence in Dudley, which grew continually. The King, and very naturally, never seems to have greatly cared for men who had ramifying bodies of support. Like the two great ministers, Dudley had nowhere to look for support but to his master.

Sir John Dudley had held various small positions. He had been cupbearer to Archbishop Cranmer at Queen Anne's coronation. He had brought in the gifts to the Queen's chamber when the Princess Elizabeth was christened. These were just enough to show that he was still about his sovereign's Court. And then in 1537 he had become Vice-Admiral. This was an office that had been held for the previous twelve years by his stepfather, Lord Lisle. A flood of information now survives about this early period of Dudley's life. It is characteristic of the early sixteenth century that all Lisle's correspondence was impounded when a charge of treason was brought against him as Governor of Calais. This contains a number of Dudley's letters.

While the Lisles and Dudleys were both isolated couples in that strange Court, their outlook on essential questions was quite remote from one another. Dudley was above all a soldier, insular in his approaches and wholly loyal to his master's policy. Lisle was very different. A man of much weaker character, he also had a strain of attachment to the old religion. He had subterranean contacts with the French nobles in Northern France; his daughter was secretly married to a cadet of the House of Montmorency. These preferences and views were not compatible with his holding a high official post under the English Crown. This explains how Dudley was not affected by the storm of fire that was to burst out over the Pale of Calais.

IV

The Pale of Calais

Lord Lisle had taken over the post of Governor of Calais in 1533 and three years later had received in addition the Lord Wardenship of the Cinque Ports. He had married a second wife shortly before receiving the earlier of these appointments. She was Lady Bassett, the guardian for her infant son of the estate of Tehidy in Cornwall; she was by birth a Grenville. A managing woman, she combined a strong vein of Catholic piety with a determination to succeed at the English Court.

These were the last days in which a close relationship was maintained with Paris. Thus Lady Lisle received letters from her English and French correspondents, John Bekinshaw and Guillaume le Métail, who were at this time in the French capital. 'I have sought,' wrote the former, 'all the goldsmiths and jewellers in Paris for your pearls and they say that you will not get hold as many in all Paris as you desire.[1] Ten merchants of the Staple [of Calais] offer me the clerk's room. I desire your counsel what I should do?' The second letter is similar in tone. 'I am now,' wrote Le Métail, 'at Court making some things for the Duchess of Etampes.'[2] He sends two crapes for Lady Lisle's daughter and for herself two thousand pins. John Hussey sent her from London a box of treacle.

There was a constant contact with the neighbouring territories. French wine was bought at Abbeville and there were complaints that the carter from Dunkirk was kept waiting at the door to the Basse Cour of Calais Castle. There was an indiscreet correspondence with French Catholics. Thus Madame de Saveuses informed Lady Lisle of a *Religieuse* who wished to live as a recluse with the

[1] *Letters & Papers, Henry VIII, vol. xiv, part ii*, 30 August 1539, p. 27.
[2] *ibid*, 27 August 1539, p. 26.

Hospitallers at Calais.[1] She was forty-eight years of age and was now at Thérouanne.

There were gifts sent to London, a basket of figs and a cask laden with twenty gallons of Malavasy wine. In November Thomas Cromwell, the Lord Privy Seal, was given a set of thirteen pieces, hangings of verdure with water flowers. Hussey has a note on this last present. 'My Lord Privy Seal thanks you, but the bringer was not so well rewarded as I thought he should have been.'[2] One has the sense that matters were not at ease for the Governor of Calais and for his wife.

During her first marriage Lady Lisle had lived a peaceful life surrounded by her high cousinage in the West of England; but now her present husband held the great fortress on the borders of the kingdom. There was naturally a myriad of spies; they were embedded in her *entourage* or lurked about her kitchens. The post in any case was rather difficult. Lord Russell, the King's new agent in the West Country, who was so wise in his relations with her kinsfolk, made this quite clear. The lord deputyship of Calais was a post which he had avoided. There were many things amiss with this English citadel when Lord Lisle came to it.

There was a constant come-and-go of travellers from France and Flanders. There were four entrances to the town of Calais, the Lantern gate towards Dunkirk, the Milk gate, the Boulogne gate and the Water gate. These gates were opened on summer mornings at five o'clock and in winter after the first striking of the watch bell, when dawn had come.[3] The burgesses kept watch upon the Castle Hill and the gates were manned by soldiers and by the servants of the Staple merchants. Places at Calais, even those with small remuneration, had been long for sale. Some were kept vacant and the income from these appropriated. There were also two hundred boys whose names were entered for a consideration as parts of the different retinues. No order was kept as to the foreigners, who came into the town. Although it had been agreed that the merchants of the Staple should give 4d on every sack of wool towards a system of countermining to defend the town, this work had been suspended for many years.

[1] *ibid*, 31 October 1539, p. 149.
[2] *ibid*, 26 November 1539, p. 208.   [3] *ibid*, p. 277.

We can picture the setting of Calais Castle as Lord Lisle's term of office was drawing to a close. In the first half of the sixteenth century it is only a catastrophe which can give us a revelation. An inventory was made on Lisle's departure.[1] One is first struck by the appurtenances of the private chapel. There was a front for the altar of cloth of gold paned with crimson velvet, which seems to have been kept for feasts. There were five plain altar cloths and a little table of the crucifix embroidered. There was, likewise, embroidery for the altar with the Bourchier knots and some of Lord Bourchier's candlesticks.[2] These had belonged to the former governor. There was a little table, which means I think a painting, of Our Lady.

My Lord's chamber had tapestry and four new Turkey carpets for cupboards, a wainscot bedstead with a canopy paned with cloth of gold and crimson satin. There was a quilt of blue and red sarcenet with a pair of fustian blankets. In the chamber out of this room there was a truckle bed, a pair of blankets of Flemish make and a close stool for a jakes.

My Lady's chamber was more elaborate. Besides a bedstead with a canopy of tawny velvet and blue satin and on the bed a pair of fustian blankets, there was also a good deal of furniture. This included a feather bed with bolsters, a cushion of satin of Bruges, a cushion of old cloth of gold, a Flanders chair. There were also nine pieces of tapestry and five curtains, these last presumably for my Lady's bed. The room also contained a great Bible, the only book that is mentioned in the house. There were also two gentlewomen's chambers and the maidens' chamber, the latter with hangings of red say.

My Lady's dining chamber (but it seems likely that it was the Lord Deputy's) was furnished with tapestry, a Turkey carpet for the board and carpets for the cupboard and the window. There was a chair covered with crimson velvet, six joined stools, twenty-eight cushions on forms set beside a long table with trestles. On the walls there was a painted cloth of Holofernes.

[1] *ibid*, pp. 24–5. An inventory made on 7 July 1540 of the contents of the house lately held by Lord Lisle in Calais.
[2] In a vestment cupboard there was one set of blue velvet with a gold cross and others of crimson velvet. There was a set of black velvet vestments in the counter and altar cloths of yellow sarcenet in the garderobe, *ibid*, p. 25.

Lord Lisle's jewellery consisted of a chain with 198 links and another gold chain, black enamelled, with 252. There was also a gold hawthorn with twenty diamonds, and a gold rose with four diamonds and three pearls. His Lordship's clothes were what one would expect, Parliament robes and then a tawny Caffa damask faced with black cony, a black satin guarded with black velvet, an old fur of Pampilion, a night petticoat of white. There follows a list of Lady Lisle's dresses. The nursery was empty save for a very old worn hanging. There was a supply of harness in the stable, some came from Naples.

In this list there is a constant reference to 'My Lady'. No mention is made of the guest chambers where the gentlemen of standing would be accommodated when they could not cross to England because the seas were boisterous. There was a constant background of moving shipping. As many as six hundred voyages were made each year into the port of Calais and the wool fleet numbered no less than sixty ships. Some London vessels made the journey as often as twelve times a year[1] bringing in wood and English beer. Twenty-four ships were registered at Calais. The fishing fleet was very numerous. There were over three hundred herring boats which came in yearly.

The religious situation was ill-controlled. From some of the parishes Papist priests had not yet been extruded, while on the other hand there was an influx of Sacramentaries, men of the new religion, come in from the Low Countries. Lord Lisle could never leave well alone. It was prudent to dissolve the Carmelite house at Calais and to obtain its lands for his own use, but it was foolish to remain on terms of friendship with the Prior. Among the priests passing through the town was Sir Gregory Buttall, who stayed at the Rose in Calais and obtained a recommendation from Lord Lisle to Bourbourg Abbey outside Gravelines. At that town he lodged at the Crown. According to information reaching London his intention was to stay with Cardinal Pole, the King's sworn enemy. All this was very dangerous.

Lord Lisle seems to have had no friends and his wife's relations were Cornish gentry with purely local influence. Lady Lisle had an intimacy with the Countess of Rutland and also a contact both

[1] *ibid*, p. 283.

with 'the old and the young Lady Marquesse of Dorset'. With this one exception neither the husband nor the wife could penetrate to the great men of the Court. And this Dorset relationship had not itself much serious value. It was during these years that the parents of Lady Jane Grey were growing up. Henry, third Marquess of Dorset, had inherited his titles and estates on his father's death in 1530, when he was a boy of thirteen. His mother had taken her place in the coronation procession of Queen Anne Boleyn and the young Marquess had first appeared at Court when carrying the salt at the christening of the Princess Elizabeth. An unconsummated marriage with Lady Catherine FitzAlan had been set aside and at the King's desire the Marquess had married his master's niece, Lady Frances Brandon, who was the elder daughter of the Duke of Suffolk. It is evident that Henry VIII, who had the companions of his own choice, had never cared for him. During these years, and he was thirty when King Henry died, Dorset received no offices, nor any of those titular dignities, the new lord lieutenancies are an example, which might have been held to be his due.

There is very little known about his life; but it seems probable that it was in this run of years that his Protestant interests were cautiously developed. Lady Jane was born at Bradgate in Leicestershire in October 1537. She was of no importance at this time for Lord Dorset was hoping for a son. In a situation in which the nobility was polarized around the Court, there was little interest shown in those who notably lacked the sovereign's favour.

From time to time in the Lisle correspondence there are references to Sir John Dudley. There are negotiations about lands at Wootton Basset and a letter to Cromwell from Dudley asking him to help him to obtain the constableship of Kenilworth. Throughout this time Dudley was careful to preserve himself; this he would always do until power came to him. He had a quick feeling for what was perilous. He had more sense than his stepfather and less religious feeling than his stepfather's wife.

Meanwhile the dangers were to some extent concealed by the great visitors in transit from time to time. Philip of Bavaria, the Count Palatine alternatively called the PfalzGraf, came through on a journey to the English Court. Lord Lisle crossed the Channel with him. By mistake the PfalzGraf left behind at Calais a bottle of walnut water, which he used to bathe his eyes. And then arrangements were made to receive the Princess of Cleves on her way to her English wedding. She rode in accompanied by the ambassadors of Cleves and Saxony and attended by some thirty trumpeters. They brought a double drum, which had not before been seen in England. Out in Calais Roads the royal ships lay dressed overall with a hundred banners of silk and gold.

Sir John Dudley was now Master of the Horse to the new Queen, and, through Lady Rutland's aid, Katharine Bassett had been named a Maid of Honour. The Princess embarked from the water steps beside the Lantern gate. This was the last act of Lord Lisle as governor. These details show that cold and empty fortress, Calais Castle.

Lord Lisle and his wife were soon brought to the Tower of London. They did not stay there long. Cromwell fell from power and he had started their prosecution. Lord Lisle was ordered to be released; but he died before this could be effected. His wife for a time went out of her mind. This was the end of Arthur Plantagenet, who had the misfortune to be a son of Edward IV, that is to say a bastard of the wrong royal House. The viscounty was conferred on the heir-of-line, Sir John Dudley.

V

The Lord Admiral

In 1542 Sir John Dudley, now Viscount Lisle, became one of the leading figures in the field of English history, a position that he would hold throughout his life. He was a man of great courage and such men inspire, sometimes unconsciously, fear in their contemporaries. By nature he belonged to the world of the *condottieri*, one of those great mercenary soldiers who were always ready to act upon the side of politics. Lisle was then, as he was to remain, essentially solitary.

He held for three months the position of Warden of the Scottish Marches and in January 1543 was promoted to the great office of Lord Admiral. He was already a privy councillor and soon became a Knight of the Garter. He had arrived. Lord Lisle was at the opening of his buoyant forties; he would remain for eleven years at the centre of power; then he would die at the early age of fifty-one. It was the last quiet period of Henry's reign. In the summer of this year he married his sixth wife, Catherine Parr. The chief characteristic shared by his last great ministers was that all of them were very isolated.

The King's health was failing; the emotional excitements of his life were over. He was gathering about him the men in whom he now had confidence; these included the Viscount Lisle. Among the principal officers of State were the members of one high family whose time of influence was over, the House of Howard, the old Duke of Norfolk and his elder son, the poet Surrey. The King disliked the elder man and had begun to distrust the younger one. They had failed and with them the Bishop of Winchester, their ally, in bringing forward Catherine Howard, to be the King's fifth Queen. It had been a bungled effort, the promoters of this affair had worked without a sufficient knowledge of the character of their *protégée*. When Catherine Howard fell, the Duke of Norfolk and his son were sealed for their own disaster. They had no connexion with Lord Lisle and the new world. In fact when Norfolk, but not his son, looked around for some ally, he had decided to choose the Seymours. Edward Seymour was to be the key figure in Dudley's rise to power.

Edward Seymour, who was at this time the Earl of Hertford and would later become the Protector Somerset, had been known to Dudley ever since they both came to Henry's Court. They had been together in France in the Duke of Suffolk's service. There had been, more recently, a law suit about some lands in Somerset which both men claimed. Still they had no more links than the long service of the same royal master. In character they were very different. Lord Hertford was a large man, tall and with a flowing flaxen beard. By birth he was the eldest son of a family of the Wiltshire squirearchy. He was friendly and easy, life had gone smoothly with him. He had had to exercise a certain dissimulation for he had early adopted a strain of Calvinist thought, which he had had the prudence to conceal. In this way he was like so many of the Court humanists of his own day, like Sir John Cheke and Anthony Cooke and Ascham. Their humanism was always visible, it was their Reformed sentiments which lay concealed.

It has always seemed strange to me that the Earl of Surrey should so much have contemned the Seymour family. They were prosperous and very long established and through his mother, who was one of the Wentworths of Nettlestead, Hertford was descended from the high stocks of the North Country. It may perhaps have been that the Wentworths, coming from the southern parts of Suffolk, rather kept themselves apart from the numerous East Anglian gentry who were linked in one way or another with the Howard affinity.

Hertford was always most approachable, but it is true that he himself was as remote as Dudley was from the great families. He had also difficulties of his own. He had five brothers and one of them, Thomas, was a thrusting fellow. What he lacked was true strength of character. His rise had been conditioned by a single

factor that he was the eldest brother of a Queen-consort, Jane
Seymour. Hertford had also had troubles in his married life.

Hertford had married when he came of age Catherine, the
daughter of a country neighbour, Sir William Fillol; but he put
her away on the grounds of her adultery with her father-in-law.
There were two sons whose paternity he did not accept, although
they were brought up in his family. His second wife was Anne,
the daughter and heiress of Sir Edward Stanhope of Rampton in
Nottinghamshire by his wife Elizabeth Bourchier, the younger
sister of the Earl of Bath. She was an arrogant and a dominating
woman. His first wife had died years before and he had now a
second family of two sons and four daughters. His wife was rather
older than himself, faithful and a heavy burden to him. The
Bourchiers were a strange stock and she took after them.

Beside these complications, there was another element which
would work to Lord Hertford's disadvantage. During the reigns
of the Tudors the great offices of State held by laymen all involved
in wartime some military command: the Lord Admiral, the Earl
Marshal, the Lord Great Chamberlain, and naturally the Wardens
of the Scottish Marches. Of course it is hard to analyse the military
skill of such an Elizabethan figure as Dudley's son, the Earl of
Leicester, but by that time there had arisen a body of professional
captains, who would assist him when he was, for instance, on
service in the Netherlands. The younger courtiers inevitably served
their sovereign on land or sea, a tradition that lasted until the
Dutch wars of Charles II. Lord Hertford had in a military sense
no special skill. He was in fact in certain ways a great civilian
statesman. Much of the immediate future turned upon the fact
that no one in the top-flight of politics was a professional soldier
except Lord Lisle.

Further, in these last years of Henry VIII's reign there was
neither peace nor prospect of peace with Scotland. It was also a
period of war with France. It was the Lord Admiral's duty to
guard the Narrow Seas and to co-operate with the military forces
on English soil and across the Channel at Calais and at Boulogne,
which was occupied by the English in these years. Given the
situation at that time, the high command was passed about between the Lord Admiral, the Lord Great Chamberlain and the

Earl of Surrey representing the Earl Marshal, who in spite of his great age was nominally the Captain General.

The office of Lord Admiral was from one aspect a great post of state in the three western monarchies. The connexion with the sea was sometimes nominal as in the case of the admirals of Castile and in the high career of the *amiral* de Coligny. At the English Court the practice sometimes varied. Thus, under Henry VIII, Sir William Fitzwilliam, later Earl of Southampton, had seen service throughout the reign and had been Vice-Admiral of England from 1513 until his appointment as Lord Admiral in 1536. He was Lord Admiral for only four years, but his portrait shows him holding the staff of his rank and at his back the sea.

At the other extreme Henry VIII's natural son, Henry Fitzroy, Duke of Richmond, became Lord Admiral in 1526 at the age of six and held the post until he died of consumption at seventeen. It seems that except for the actual purposes of sea warfare, the Lord Admiral very seldom went afloat. The ships of those days were not built to accommodate a high commander. The great cabin of the *Ark Royal* in which Lord Howard of Effingham took counsel, belonged to the conditions of the later part of the century. The Spanish galleons carrying the viceroys to the Pacific appear to have been the first big ships with what we should regard as permanent passenger accommodation.

Lord Lisle sailed in the *Henry Grace à Dieu*. It was natural that he should make her his flagship. She was the largest naval vessel, dating from the beginning of the reign and recently rebuilt. He cruised in the Channel in her and assisted at the attack on Boulogne. He was also on board her when d'Annebaut made his approach to Portsmouth and his attack upon the Isle of Wight.

The members of the Naval service had as yet but little solidarity. Among the serving captains of this time, however, there were two who would in time reach supreme command, Lord William Howard, father of Howard of Effingham of the Armada, and Lord Clinton; but there were no links between them and neither in any case belonged to Lisle's affinity. The post of Lord High Admiral was a great Court appointment, held only by a small range of high officers who had the sovereign's personal support. It raised Lord Lisle to a position of much influence; but it could always be

regarded as a stepping stone to a yet higher place. It did not serve
to distract his mind from the command of the land forces in the
realm of England.

During the period of his term of office there were various changes
in the structure of the Naval administration which are generally
attributed to William Gonson, who had long held the office of
Surveyor of the Ships, and to the members of his family. If that
be the case the *rôle* of Lord Lisle falls into place; for Lisle understood the man at arms, whether a seaman or a soldier. He was on
easy terms, too, with the type of merchant who hired armed men
to make his voyages.

From 1544 he had the uneasy collaboration of Lord Hertford's
brother, Sir Thomas Seymour, as Vice-Admiral. When the King
died the latter was created a peer and Sir William Paget stated
that it was the late sovereign's wish that he should be made Lord
Admiral. Lord Lisle had received this appointment for life, but
on this assertion he gave it up. In later life he showed great interest in voyages of discovery. To the Admiralty he did not return.

Why did he not return to the Admiralty in later life, when all
the offices beneath the Crown were open to him? It seems to me
that as he went up the winding stair he passed the point where the
great post of Lord Admiral was any service.

VI

The King's Will

Henry VIII was slowly dying. There were various possibilities for
the regency which would rule England until Edward reached the
age of eighteen in the autumn of 1555. In the first place the King
could have appointed his elder daughter, the Lady Mary, who
was now thirty, as Regent for her young stepbrother. This step
would not have been unprecedented for in the previous century
Anne de Beaujeu had been Regent of France for her brother
Charles VIII, who was a minor. It would, however, have been
impracticable. The royal Regent would have had the right to
choose her ministers. The question of the King's marriage with the
Princess of Aragon would have been re-opened; the influence of
Spain would have seeped in; the Lady Mary would in time have
overturned the King's religious settlement.

Henry VIII's younger daughter, the Lady Elizabeth, was a girl
of thirteen, and both his sisters were now dead. The relatives of the
sovereign were all scattered. The Marchioness of Exeter and her
son, Lord Courtenay, were prisoners in the Tower of London. The
leader of the Poles, the Cardinal of Santa Maria in Cosmedin, was
abroad, an exile. Among what may in a broad sense be considered
the King's relatives were two leading peers, the Marquess of Dorset
and the Earl of Hertford. Henry Grey and his family had been
close to their sovereign throughout the last reign and the King had
in fact arranged his marriage. The Marchioness of Dorset was the
elder daughter of the late Duke of Suffolk by his marriage with the
Queen of France, the King's sister. Henry VIII, whose knowledge of men was on a certain level quite acute, did not consider
him. He understood the weakness of his character. That left the

Earl of Hertford, who was the brother of Jane Seymour and thus the young prince's uncle.

There were also the King's two remaining relatives by marriage, the brother and the brother-in-law of Queen Catherine, his last wife. Lord Parr, who had been created Earl of Essex in 1543, had married the daughter and heiress of the last holder of the Bour- chier earldom. Before the King's death she had eloped from him, but Parr retained her great estates and property. He does not seem to have been a very happy or ultimately a successful man. Like his sister he was a convinced Protestant.

Sir William Herbert, the scion of an illegitimate branch of the Earls of Pembroke of the first creation, was already wealthy having gained the great estates of Wilton Abbey. He was married to Catherine Parr's younger sister. Neither of these men belonged to the educated section of the peerage, but Herbert had a truly admirable tenacity. Upon both of them Lord Lisle's influence would come to play. It must, however, be stressed that Hertford, Essex and Sir William Herbert were all related to the King's wise queens, Jane Seymour and Catherine Parr.

At the very end of the reign there took place the destruction of the House of Howard. They had long been to the north of the old King's favour. In the actual circumstances the Duke of Norfolk was brought down by his son Surrey. On 12 December 1546 they were arrested together, but their trials were separate. Surrey was condemned and executed for quartering his shield as if he were the heir apparent to the Crown, and for stating that his father would one day rule England for the young prince. Norfolk unloaded, and quite justly, the blame upon his son and stressed the wish that he had expressed for marriage alliances with the Seymour family. Nevertheless, a bill of attainder was passed against him and was waiting for the royal assent when the King died. From among the claimants to power the House of Howard was now eliminated.

From many points of view the reign of Edward VI, which was soon to open, should be regarded as a period of eclipse of Tudor kingship. The royal power to execute great men and to confiscate their properties was in abeyance. As an example, the Duke of Norfolk was never to suffer execution. Although both the admini- strations of the Duke of Somerset and the Duke of Northumberland had elements of the dictatorships, they were, from another angle, a period of oligarchic rule. Only one great man would ever suffer execution in King Edward's reign, and in that case it would appear improbable that capital punishment would ever have been inflicted on the Duke of Somerset if he had not beheaded Lord Seymour, his own brother.

What was needed to make an oligarchic government lastingly successful was a careful balancing of power, a combination of adroitness and of skill. It would be unfortunate for Northumberland that he had only one answer to every problem and that was the use of *force*. True he inspired fear but that alone was in the last resource quite ineffective.

The greater peers were in a sense all equals. No man had any right to take away from them their great and, for the most part, recently acquired possessions. They had no practice in the making of combinations. If there was one lesson that King Henry taught them all, it was that no man could combine against the Crown.

It was a further difficulty for Lord Lisle that all the future honours would be bestowed by a King, who was a minor.

While there seems to have been expectation of the appointment of a single individual as Regent, the main effect of Henry VIII's will was to hand over the function of a Regency to the Privy Council. It was no surprise that the name of the Bishop of Winchester was excluded. As to the royal attitude towards the Bishop, we have the King's words to Sir Anthony Browne, reported by Sir Anthony Denny on the not very good authority of Foxe. 'I remembered him well enough,' explained the sovereign, 'and of good purpose have left him out [from the list of my executors]; for surely if he was in my testament and one of you, he would cumber you all, and you should never rule him, he is of so troublesome a nature. . . . I myself could use him, and rule him to all manner of purposes, as seemed good unto me; but so shall you never do.'[1] For the rest the use of the Privy Council excluded from the Regency all the members of the old peerage with the single exception of the Earl of Arundel, whose position will be considered later.

There was obviously a great disparity of authority between the

[1] Cf. Foxe, *Acts and Monuments*, v, pp. 91-2.

various members since the Privy Council included a number of comparatively junior officials. These were such men as Sir Anthony Wingfield, the Vice-Chamberlain, Sir Ralph Sadler, Master of the Wardrobe, Sir Edmund Peckham, Treasurer of Calais, and Sir Anthony Denny. Such names will not recur again. It was the leaders of the Privy Council who alone would carry weight. As a matter of fact this situation of a widespread Regency never came into force; but it is as well to consider here the one protagonist of the King's wishes, Thomas Lord Wriothesley, the Chancellor and Earl of Southampton.

Like many members of the new Tudor aristocracy his family was accustomed to the Court, his father being York herald and his uncle and grandfather both Garter kings-of-arms. He was an early disciple of Thomas Cromwell and did much secretarial work for him. He was, indeed, one of the principal beneficiaries of Cromwell's policies. He was known as a great, perhaps the greatest of the sixteenth-century accumulators. His fortune was wholly built upon monastic land. In the days when the monasteries were falling he lived at Micheldever in a house, which now has disappeared, on the southern lip of that great windy downland which lies to the southward of Andover and Basingstoke. Beyond him lay the county of Southampton, which would give its title to his earldom, and there lay the rich lands which would come to him, the former wide possessions of the abbeys of Titchfield and Beaulieu and Hyde at Winchester, which he would pull down. His work was unremitting and he was tenacious. In London he built Southampton House in Holborn, which had been the town residence of the Bishops of Ely, and acquired the manor or grange of Bloomsbury. He was appointed Joint Secretary of State in 1540 and promoted almost by chance to the chancellorship four years later. Like Cromwell, he had a gift for following the King's intentions.

A. F. Pollard sees his return to Catholicism about 1540; but I can find no evidence of this. He was to some extent in foreign policy a pro-Imperialist and he had no sympathy with the Hot Gospellers. We can understand that acquisition would make a man conservative. But we can now see better than the nineteenth-century English historians could do, a man who is indifferent to religion can dislike a noisy proclamation of Old Testament values as heartily as any Papist. The Earl of Southampton's concerns were always bound up with the kingdoms of this world.

It is worth remembering Southampton for he was in some ways typical. Except for Paulet and Russell, who were born at the beginning of the reign of Henry VII, the future ministers were of an age, already in the early forties. Henry VIII did not care for younger men. They had therefore made their fortunes. They were circumspect and careful, except for Lisle. The Howards alone had had a great affinity and throughout the coming reign they would be powerless. The rest, speaking in rather general terms, had neither ancestors, nor relatives. Each man was isolated. Their rise had made them solitary. It was a consequence of their success that each man had constructed his own pyramid. They were linked by a single quality which was in no sense a uniting force; they all were swift and pliant to serve the King. And this was why they had been chosen by their master.

One alone among them was very different. Henry FitzAlan, twelfth Earl of Arundel, was the solitary member of the greater peers on the Council of Regency. He was thirty-five, a rather younger man than all his colleagues. He was a godson of King Henry and had been about the Court since a small boy. The rich young Lord Maltravers seems to have been a *protégé* both of the old Cardinal and of the King. The FitzAlans had a relatively small accretion of monastic property, the priory of Michelham and lands which had belonged to Lewes.

In doctrinal matters he appeared indifferent or to put it more exactly he always accepted the religion of the Court. Owing to the Catholic *cultus* for his grandson we happen to possess the exact details of his allegiances.[1] But what really mattered was his devotion to the monarchy; he had a conservative attachment to the Crown of England.

Lord Arundel's mother had been a daughter of Lord Northumberland, but the Percy family were under attainder until after

---

[1] Arundel was an Henrican Catholic and then nominally a Protestant. He returned to Catholicism under Mary and in her sister's reign was an Anglican of a conservative mould. Shortly before his death in 1580 he was reconciled to the Church of Rome by a priest brought him by his son-in-law Lord Lumley. Cf. *The Right Honourable the Lady Anne Countess Arundel* (wife of Philip Earl of Arundel) ed. by the Duke of Norfolk in 1857, p. 177.

King Edward's death. He began as a young man with a grand
alliance. At twenty-one he married Lady Catherine Grey, while
his sister Lady Catherine FitzAlan married his new brother-in-law,
the Marquess of Dorset. This latter marriage was soon annulled;
but there seems no reason to suppose that he bore resentment
against the Dorset family. His second wife, whom Arundel had at
this date married recently, was widow to the Earl of Sussex and a
daughter of Sir John Arundell of Lanherne. The Earl now held the
great office of Lord Great Chamberlain. A small, compact man
with wide-set eyes, he was a somewhat inactive figure in that
thrusting age.

Sir William Paget, who had been Secretary of State since 1543
and was also joint Chancellor of the Duchy of Lancaster, was the
official of the second rank who was most deeply concerned with
the King's will. He had long attached himself to Lord Hertford.
He was in favour of acting with caution and, in particular, he
deprecated any rapid change in altering the King's settlement of
religion. He was rising to some wealth and he had obtained the
areas of church land on which he was eventually to erect his house
at Beaudesert, on the uplands near the edge of Cannock Chase. He
had a long plain face.[1] He was in one sense an important figure
for it fell to him to convey to the Council as soon as the King was
dead his last intentions. These were the grants of titles, lands and
pensions which were intended to anchor the favoured courtiers in
loyalty to their young sovereign.

By this arrangement the Earl of Hertford was to be created
Duke of Somerset, the Earl of Essex Marquess of Northampton,
and the Viscount Lisle and Lord Wriothesley would receive the
earldoms of Coventry and Southampton. Lisle in fact preferred the
Warwick title. Sir William Herbert would receive a little later the
earldom of Pembroke. It will be seen that provision had been made
for the King's relatives. Similar promotions were offered to Lord
St John of Basing and Lord Russell, who refused them for the
moment, but who, later in 1551 and 1550, became the Earls of
Wiltshire and Bedford. These were two elder statesmen, who held

---

[1] There are two surviving portraits, one by an unknown hand at Plas Newydd and the
other at the National Portrait Gallery attributed to the Master of the Stätthalterin
Madonna. Cf. Roy Strong, *Tudor and Jacobean Portraits*, i, p. 241.

the offices of Lord Steward and Lord Privy Seal. Sir Thomas Seymour became Lord Seymour of Sudeley. These were the names under which the principal leaders would be known henceforward. Lord Southampton would soon die and both the Seymours would be executed. The others would plough on throughout Edward's short reign.

Although all these great men were independent there were some who took but very little action. An example is William Paulet, Lord St John of Basing, who became Earl of Wiltshire and then Marquess of Winchester. In the course of the reign he moved from the office of Lord Steward to that of the treasurership of the Kingdom. His life was the quintessence of wisdom as the Tudor generations understood this. It was not his practice to write down his thoughts. His private archives have not survived. We do not even know the nature of Basing House as he constructed it. This mansion, with the changes that his successors made in it, perished in the Civil Wars in the succeeding century. Everything now lies under the curving mounds of grass eastwards from Basingstoke. We cannot say very much beyond the fact that he had a pristine reverence for the Tudor monarchy.

The first struggle of the new reign was to be between the Duke of Somerset and the Earl of Warwick, who would then emerge as sole ruler and Duke of Northumberland. The Marquess of Dorset would in time be numbered among the leadership and also the Earl of Shrewsbury. This concludes the whole list of the *Dramatis Personae*, as far as the lay leaders were concerned.

VII

The New Reign

The new reign opened under the Protectorate of the Duke of Somerset. His promotion to the dukedom had made that possible. There were at that time only two others of that rank in England; they held the long-familiar titles of Norfolk and Suffolk. Their position left the Duke of Somerset in 1547 without a rival. Norfolk was a tired and very old man who remained throughout the reign, without much discomfort, in the Tower of London; the other was a boy. The old Duke of Suffolk had died in 1545 and had left two sons, who in turn succeeded to the title. These were the only children of his last wife, the half-Spanish Catherine Willoughby, whom he had married when he was widowed of the Queen of France. They were brought up in their mother's strict Protestantism and the elder was now a boy of twelve. In 1551 they were both, though very young to be undergraduates, at St John's College, Cambridge. That summer the sweating sickness broke out in the town and they were removed to the Bishop of Lincoln's palace at Buckden in Lincolnshire. They caught the sickness and both died there; the younger survived the elder by half an hour.

Somerset is often described as an idealist in the nineteenth-century understanding of that word, bent upon the curing of social disorders. There is, however, no reason to suppose that he possessed a social conscience in the modern sense. This could hardly be found in Tudor England. The basis of his outlook was his religion. The new Protestantism, which he had adopted, had given him a feeling for all men whose minds were open to the hearing of God's Word. In consequence he was among the very few men of his high rank who had a feeling for the new urban Protestants and for those

who shared their views among the rural poor. To those of his own
world all this was moonshine.

I doubt if he realized how far removed he was from his own
class. He was in fact surrounded by hard-headed men. He had no
friends, his greatest danger was from his brother, and his wife was
an encumbrance. Still, although he had no friends he had a
manager, Sir William Paget. Beyond that portrait with the great
nose and the ginger hair it is hard for us to penetrate. We know
very little of Paget for he was a man who aimed at power, but
never gained it.

It may seem strange that Somerset should become Protector if
he had no friendship or alliance; but Paget had a working mind
and there was no man among the Council who was the equal of
one who combined a dukedom with being the maternal uncle to
his young sovereign. At any rate they voted for him. The first
episode of the new *régime* was a simple matter, the removal of the
new Earl of Southampton, who had opposed the notion of a Protectorate; he sickened in retirement and soon died. As his heir was
still a little boy, this meant the end of the Wriothesley family as
an element of power throughout this reign. He was succeeded by
Lord Rich, who held the chancellorship for just four years. He was
an accomplished lawyer and a devoted servant of his late royal
master. He had inherited a mercantile fortune and he gained
another, brought him by his wife. He had obtained much monastic land, in particular the estates of Lees Priory in Essex, which he
pulled down and then rebuilt as his own residence. A certain
quietness marked him for he had come in on favouring tides. Still
this change was not important, it was Sir Thomas Seymour who
provided the first real problem.

Meanwhile Somerset took over, almost unconsciously, the great
offices of the kingdom. He became Earl Marshal, one of the posts
laid down by the Duke of Norfolk. He became Lord Treasurer; he
was elected Chancellor of Cambridge University. And then he was
so quiet. His Calvinism was in part responsible for his lack of ostenta-
tion. The half-length portrait at Longleat by an unknown painter,
one of the only two surviving portraits, brings this out clearly.[1]

[1] This portrait is here reproduced (Plate 2). The other picture is a miniature by
Nicholas Hilliard painted in 1560 from an original now lost.

D

He wears on his head a wide and low black hat relieved by a small circlet of sparkling diamonds sewn on below the brim. There is a small white pleated ruff above the long black gown and against this the gold work of the Garter chain. This brings a touch of Geneva, and then the deep-sunk eyes in the white face, with their look of unsuitable tranquillity, by far too tranquil for that cruel age. Imagination is what the Duke so sadly lacked.

Curiously enough one of the few pictures described as representing his brother Thomas was also at Longleat. This was used by Lodge and is in consequence familiar.[1] He is represented as a fine figure of a man with a great beard. He was not slow in seeking for promotion. He was created Lord Seymour of Sudeley and received the Garter, and was then made Lord Admiral. It was not very prudent to take away John Dudley's post and to give it to his former subordinate. In the early summer of 1547 Lord Seymour married Catherine Parr, the Queen Dowager.

Lord Paget had given it as his opinion that no changes should be made in religious matters in the new reign. His views were always those of the *politiques*, like them his one desire in times of turmoil was to build up the monarchy. There was also something to be said for the point of view, which Bishop Gardiner represented, that changes in the religious life of England should not be made while the head of the Church was still a minor.

The reign inevitably opened under the religious arrangements which were the legacy of the late sovereign. It was only the space of a short thirteen years since the Henrican Catholic system had been established. King Henry had disliked all novelty and there was nothing very fresh as the ritual went forward a trifle heavily; the man who had devised it now lay dead. The fulfilment of the King's bequests was just beginning, those masses for the repose of his soul which should be celebrated in a chapel at Windsor Castle 'for evermore'. During the whole of the first year of the new reign the accustomed masses had been kept up at the Court;[2] the feast of Corpus Christi and those of the Apostles and then that cluster of Marian feasts which marked the Nativity and the Conception and

---

[1] Printed in Lodge's *Portraits*, vol. i, in 1835 and then attributed to Holbein.
[2] Cf. preface to *The Literary Remains of Edward VI* by John Gough Nichols, Roxburghe Society (1857), vol. i, p. xcix.

the Assumption of Our Blessed Lady. One may imagine they were attended languidly, but the changes now came about still very slowly. Even towards the end of December when Edward VI kept his celebration at Hampton Court, there was still an item for the children of the King's Chapel, for singing *Gloria in Excelsis* on Christmas Day.[1]

At Westminster the great church was preparing for the coronation; the choir was now made rich with hangings of Arras against the walls; the smoothed paving stones were laid with rushes. The trumpets blew as the three crowns in succession were set upon the young King's head. A ring of gold was placed upon His Grace's marrying finger. The choir sang the *Te Deum*; the organ played.

One can see him as he came up the aisle, a boy of ten. He was a quiet and studious child with a built-in distaste for all Church ceremonies. Alone of all his family, his clothes meant nothing to him. He probably hardly saw the light reflected from his jewellery. He did not like flattery; he was nourished on the Word of God.

They had made him ready for a gorgeous ceremonial. At the main door his horse was waiting, a patient beast, 'with a caparison of crimson satin embroidered with pearls and damasked gold'. King Edward had been dressed with splendour. He had a gown of cloth of silver with a girdle of white velvet wrought with Venice silk.[2] The gown was powdered with rubies and diamonds. Pearls were scattered on the great white velvet cloak embroidered with Venetian silver. The King was small and slender and on his feet he wore white velvet buskins. The symbols of royalty were all about him. Maltravers, Arundel's son, a boy even younger than himself, carried the insignia of the Chief Butler of England. The great peers stood around him. There was Derby bearing the mantle and on the King's right, Shrewsbury with the rod of gold. On his other side was Oxford with the Crown. Arundel bore one Sword of State and Huntingdon the other. Sussex carried the cap with the 'cyreillet'. There was a small procession of Suffolk, Dorset, Essex and Lisle. All were resplendent in their robes of State. It was at this ceremony that Dorset came for a moment into his own.

[1] *ibid*, p. xcix.   [2] ibid, p. xcv.

He had been recognized as chief mourner at the old King's funeral. He was created Lord High Constable for three days to superintend King Edward's coronation. He also received the Garter as an attribute to his rank. Still the great office was strictly temporary, he remained in effect a forgotten man.

The focus of loyalty was indeed the Crown. The claim of the legitimate heir was quite unbreakable, whether it was that of King Henry's only son or, later, the claim of the same sovereign's elder daughter. The greater peers inevitably were drawn towards the monarchy. It was irrelevant that they had little power, for this depended on another factor, the Duke of Somerset's *camarilla*.

The religious changes of the period tend to distract attention from one of the features of the contemporary scene, the very great power which then existed in the whole institution of the Western Monarchies. The heads of the House of Tudor had a power which none could rival. The influence of the new nationalism would reinforce the English kingship.

The first two years of the Protectorate were marked by three main series of events, the development of religion, which meant leading the people towards the reformed faith, and the gradual change in the civil administration. In dealing with these two subjects the Duke showed a certain good-hearted kindness; he was much less harsh in his approach than either Queen Mary or Queen Elizabeth. Neither of these matters appears to have been of great interest to Warwick, as John Dudley had now become. But at the same time Somerset was involved in Henry VIII's foreign policy and the wars which this brought in its train.

This was Dudley's field of knowledge. He had much more experience and sense of war than any of his English contemporaries. In fact the outbreak of war inevitably created danger for any superior who lacked both Dudley's technical knowledge and his almost unbreakable determination. But this was one of the dangers that a man with the Duke of Somerset's temperament could not foresee.

In the halcyon days at the commencement of the Protectorate there were many gifts of Crown property and a proportion of sales on easy terms. The leaders were building up their great landed estates. Thus Somerset received sixty-three manors and Thomas

Seymour forty-eight. Pembroke gained fifty-one and Warwick a solid haul.[1]

Dudley had taken the name of Warwick for his earldom because he was among the heirs general to that title, which was now extinct. It was valued as one of the great earldoms of the Middle Ages. These are the details, although the claim may seem a trifle fragile. In the first place the heirship to the family had passed through the Beauchamp heiress who had married Warwick the King-maker to her granddaughter, the Countess of Salisbury. It was only on her attainder in 1539 that any claim for Dudley could have been made. He was the great-grandson of John Talbot, Viscount Lisle, the only son of the Earl of Salisbury by his second wife, Lady Margaret Beauchamp, daughter of Richard Earl of Warwick. It was on these rather difficult grounds that he obtained a grant of the lordship, manor, township and castle of Warwick.

In those days he could have had no conception of the title of Northumberland. It seems likely that when the idea of promotion came before him he thought of the dukedom of Warwick, which had been held briefly by the Beauchamps in the fifteenth century. He was early determined to take his place among the heads of the high English families. It was a point of view that was later to be reflected in the career of his son Robert, the great Earl of Leicester.

When he surrendered the post of Lord Admiral, Dudley received in exchange the office of Lord High Chamberlain. He was also given in the July after King Edward's accession, the office of Lieutenant of all the Northern Counties, and made one of the commanders of the army against the Scots. Is it ever wise to give a rival the full range of all his opportunities? The Duke of Somerset could never see the forces that were building up against him.

[1] In the course of time Warwick obtained the greatest number of any beneficiary, a total of eighty-eight manors. None of the other peers received a comparable increase. Paulet gained twenty-eight manors. These were the only men who obtained more than twenty. Cf. List printed in W. K. Jordan, *Edward the Young King*, p. 116.

I

The Rising in the West

The revolt in the West of England came as a surprise to the Duke of Somerset. He had no knowledge of those parts of his country in which his Church reforms might meet with opposition. There are various aspects of this rising which still cause surprise. It came in a part of England which was conservative enough, but in no sense strongly linked with later Catholic recusancy. Above all, there is the question of the intentions of the leadership.

Humphrey Arundell, of Helland in Cornwall, was the cadet of a house with Court connections, but he himself was a home-keeping Cornish squire of medium fortune. He was at this time thirty-six years of age and married to the daughter of a considerable landowner in the neighbouring county, Sir John Fulford of Great Fulford in Devonshire. He had reached manhood before the breach with Rome.

His cousins at Lanherne had soared above him in consequence of the marriage of his uncle, Sir John Arundell, now dead, with Lady Elizabeth Grey, one of the children of the first Marquess of Dorset. His two cousins were now both in the Court world; Sir John Arundell of Lanherne was married to Lady Anne Stanley, a sister of the Earl of Derby, and his younger brother, Sir Thomas, had obtained in 1547 a grant of Wardour Castle and its lands in the south of Wiltshire. Their half-sister, Mary Arundell, had made two great marriages and was now the wife of the Earl of Arundel. Both the Lanherne brothers were closely associated politically with the Duke of Somerset. They had held office under Henry VIII and Humphrey Arundell had received a grant of the dissolved religious house, St Michael's Mount.

It is the persistent problem in considering the three risings, the

Pilgrimage of Grace under Aske and the rebellion in Cornwall under Arundell, and that under Kett in Norfolk, as to how the leaders could imagine that they might prove successful. They were all undertaken against strong governments, the first against King Henry's, and the two last against that united body of the rich which held control during King Edward's minority. It might be said that Robert Kett because of his social inexperience was without understanding of the powers of Government, and that Robert Aske had an exaggerated notion of what the North, supported by the northern peerage, might achieve; but how could Humphrey Arundell have thought that he might be successful in Cornwall?

There is another element in the problem which appears strange. Arundell does not seem to have been in any way a specifically religious man, but he found himself in the leadership of a group which was almost exclusively concerned with the discipline of the Church. The first movement against the chantries in 1549 was without any very great results, but it is curious that the introduction of the new Prayer Book should, in the South of England have only met with serious opposition in parts of Devonshire and in the Duchy of Cornwall. North of Trent the situation was very different, but there is not as yet a study of the reception of the Prayer Book in the parishes in the northern counties. It is possible that part of the answer lies in the constitution of the diocese of Exeter, which included all the area involved.

This see had as its head the oldest of all the members of the Bench of Bishops, Dr John Veysey. He appears to have been born as long ago as 1465 and he had held the diocese of Exeter since 1521. He had, until age came upon him, been an active bishop. He was conservative and Regalian; he had been much about the Court in the first portion of King Henry's reign, Dean of Windsor and Registrar of the Order of the Garter. One episode from his past remained of value; he was now the sole survivor of the prelates who had consecrated Archbishop Cranmer. In his failing years he had retired to the manor house of Sutton Coldfield in the Midlands, which he had inherited from an uncle. He was seldom in London during this reign and his name does not appear among those who voted on Prayer Book Reform.[1]

[1] The best account of Bishop Veysey is to be found in A. L. Rowse, *Tudor Cornwall*, a most valuable study.

In the first years of his rule he had been assisted by John Vyvyan, Bishop of Megara and Prior of Bodmin. To a much greater extent than in other southern dioceses, the bulk of the parish clergy were local men, usually of farming stock from the West of England. A certain relaxation of central control had enabled them to build up a close authority over their flock.

Very early in the reign the Bishop of Winchester was removed from the scene. As Cardinal Mazarin on his death-bed left a warning against Fouquet, so had Henry VIII left a warning against Stephen Gardiner. He had soon been deprived of the chancellorship of the University of Cambridge. He had never been admitted to King Edward's Privy Council. In July 1548 he had been committed to the Tower.

It seems that both Somerset and the Archbishop were irked by the many Marian feasts which had been preserved from Henry VIII's day. Under the then law there was no way of allowing them to fall into desuetude, they must be abrogated. Further, the Archbishop's thought was constantly evolving. The most striking change lay in the fact that the whole of the Sunday service was transferred from Latin into English. Almost all the references to the saints were swept away, and also the long-accustomed ceremonies, the ashes on Ash Wednesday and the palms on Palm Sunday, the candles at Candlemas. The canon of the mass was retained; but the Lutheran implications were very clear to those who studied them. It was in many respects an *interim* statement and it was hoped that it would be accepted without difficulty by those who had been nourished on Henrican Catholicism. Among other changes the marriage of the clergy was now permitted. It was natural that it should be the conservative section of the clergy who should first object to it.

It was inevitable that the more conservative section of the Episcopate should object to these changes from the regulation of the Church set out in King Henry's time. Eight bishops voted in the minority when the Act was brought forward in the House of Lords. They were, as will be seen later, not a united opposition and seem to have had little contact with their lay supporters.

Only a tiny fragment of the lay peerage supported the bishops of the minority with their votes on this occasion. The solitary member among the greater peers was Edward, third Earl of Derby, who modified his opinions later. For the last twelve years of his life, from 1559 onwards, he was to be in active support of the Elizabethan Church order. Lord Wharton, another signatory, would also share his later outlook. Francis, fifth Earl of Shrewsbury, the leader of the Regalian Catholics, does not appear to have attended the House of Lords. For the rest, Lord Dacres was at feud with Wharton, a 'new man'; Lord Morley was very old, a man of letters, and Windsor, a supporter of the Lady Mary.

It was decided that these changes should be carried out on the following Whit Sunday. In a wholly agricultural region it was perhaps a mistake to wait until the harvest had been gathered.

In Cornwall there had been some unconnected difficulty in the previous year. William Body, Archdeacon of Cornwall, a layman and a *protégé* of Cromwell's, had been killed during an *émeute* at the house in Helston where he had been staying. It seems that the actual blows were struck of William Kilter of Constantine and Pascoe Trevian; but it was Geoffrey Martin, a mass-priest of St Keverne, who was brought to London and executed there.[1]

There was a uniform date for the beginning of the new service. For this reason all the troubles broke out together. The very first of them was in the poor parish of Sampford Courtenay on the edge of the bare moor. On Whit Monday the villagers, under the leadership of Underhill, a tailor, persuaded their priest to say mass instead of the new service. All through that week the men from different parishes in Cornwall led by their priests were marching on Bodmin, where they were joined by the mayor. They then passed eastwards by way of Tavistock until they reached the outer walls of Exeter, where the Devon men joined with them. During this time they were working out their demands under the leadership of their priests. They damaged no property as they marched eastwards. Their leaders were Humphrey Arundell and one other gentleman, John Winslade of Tregarrick. They settled down into four camps. The mayors of Bodmin and Torrington were each in charge of a camp. It is rather surprising to find the two mayors there. When men had reached to that official rank they usually had a greater prudence. The other camps were under two local

[1] A. L. Rowse, *op. cit.*, pp. 257–9.

priests, John Thompson and Roger Barrett. They were also joined by the Vicar of St Thomas's, Exe Island.

At this point they sent forward their demands. These were in fifteen articles clearly drawn up under the direction of the clergy. With one exception, they dealt with specifically religious questions. 'We will have,' they asked, 'all the general councils and holy decrees of our forefathers observed, kept and performed. We will have the laws of our sovereign lord King Henry VIII concerning the six articles to be used again as in his time they were. We will have the mass in Latin, as it was before, and celebrated by the priest without any man or woman communicating with him. We will have the sacrament hung over the high altar, and thus be worshipped as it was wont to be. We will have the sacrament of the altar but at Easter delivered to the people and then but in one kind. We will that our curate shall minister the sacrament of baptism at all times, as well on the week-days as on the holydays. We will have holy bread [blessed bread] and holy water every Sunday, palms and ashes at the time accustomed, Images to be set up again in every church, and all other ancient ceremonies held heretofore by our Holy Mother Church.'

There was also an *addendum*. 'We will have every preacher in his sermon and every priest in the mass, pray, especially by name, for the souls in Purgatory, as our forefathers did.' One section was set out with great imprudence seeing that the new instructions were a royal command. 'We will not receive the new service, because it is but like a Christmas game.' There were various references to heresy and heretics. It was stated that the Cornishmen could not understand the English prayers. There were also two personal requests. The first was that Dr Moreman and Dr Crispin, both Canons of Exeter, should be sent to them 'to preach among us our Catholic Faith'. The other was that Cardinal Pole should be promoted to the Royal Council. This was the solitary phrasing which had any contact with the Church of Rome. There was finally a wholly secular proposal that 'no gentleman should have any more servants than one to wait upon him'. It can be said that for effective purposes this all meant nothing.

Meanwhile the rising flared up for the last time. The rebels, by this time a disorganized force of about twenty thousand men, decided to invest and capture Exeter. Inside the city there was a small store of cannon; but the invaders had no armaments. These projects were pressed forward by the Vicar of St Thomas's, a church which lay outside and below the county town in the water meadows, through which the Great Western main line now runs on its way southward towards the sea.

There was a little battle by the barns of Crediton, and the road now lay open to the royal forces. The last action of the rising soon took place in the village of Sampford Courtenay, where the stir had its beginning.

One punishment was immediately inflicted. The Vicar of St Thomas's was hanged on a gallows set up against his steeple. He had been forced to put on his vestments. A holy water stoup, a sprinkler and a sacring bell were tied to him. There was nothing that could surprise him in this end. He had heard, as had all Western men, of the mock made by the baser sort of his opponents; how a dead stray dog had been hanged and in his crossed paws was placed a circular piece of hard white paper to represent the sacred Host. In general terms the Government acted with relative mercy.

How were these events likely to have been considered from the standpoint of the Protector? It is best to go back a little. Lord Russell, in command of the royal forces, was growing elderly and suffering somewhat from the gout. It was clear to him by now that his western lands had been left unmolested. He sat at his ease at Hinton St George in the wide policies of the senior line of the Paulets, whose great new house was already growing there. Sir Hugh Paulet was a soldier and a supporter of the Government. Among his children was his son Amyas who, in later years, would be the last gaoler of the Queen of Scots.

The house stood a few miles north of Crewkerne; westward lay Devonshire. The old religion vanished fast in that soft country. There were no Papists, to use that term in its wide expression, among the eastern combes or in those rich lands which lay southward between Ilminster and the sea.

Lord Russell knew of Humphrey Arundell and had heard that his cousin Sir John was now in Dorset. Russell urged him to join him; but Sir John refused. It was not wise to refuse to join the representative of the King's authority. The land-owning class, whatever some of its members' private views, was wholly loyal. He had in his company Miles Coverdale, the translator of the Bible, who was come to preach the new religion to the Western men. Lord Russell had no opinion of the old-fashioned clergy.

No man of standing could fail to understand the true position. It was lovely summer weather in the West of England. The military position was satisfactory. Sir William Herbert was approaching from Wilton with his Welsh contingent. One hundred and fifty Italian arquebusiers were on their way. There were also one thousand 'Almain' foot, mercenaries like the Italians, but this time from Western Germany. They were bringing a sledge hammer to crack a nut; but then the Duke of Somerset was no soldier.

Kestell, who had been Humphrey Arundell's secretary, surrendered just before his master. He brought charges against Sir John and Sir Thomas Arundell and they were both placed in the Tower. Humphrey Arundell and Winslade suffered at Tyburn.

There have been various views as to the military significance of this rebellion. It would seem that it was destined to failure from the first owing to the absence of effective leadership among the rebels. There was no other disturbance of the country gentry. The possessors were all left in their possession.

II

The Norfolk Rising

For a Lord Protector surrounded by envious and powerful rivals of noble birth it would usually be prudent to carry forward a foreign policy, which was both aggressive and traditional. However, one senses that the Duke of Somerset was not greatly interested in such questions. The last years of King Henry's reign had been occupied by a policy which was hostile towards those two old allies, the kingdoms of France and Scotland. In regard to France the war in time gave place to a truce which left the French town of Boulogne in English hands. There could be no true peace with France as long as this situation should endure.

The war with Scotland was endemic. It had begun in 1542, the year in which James V of Scotland died leaving an infant heir, Mary Queen of Scots. It had been Henry VIII's policy, and it was now Somerset's, that the young Queen should be married to the Prince of Wales, who had now become Edward VI. This was opposed by her mother the Queen Regent, Mary of Lorraine, and by all those Scots who were opposed to the merging of their country in the neighbouring kingdom. It remained an objective of English policy until the Queen of Scots was sent into France in 1548 as the betrothed bride of the French dauphin. The difficulties with France continued for two years longer until peace was made in 1550 and Boulogne was returned to her French inheritors, as the result of a payment of rather over £133,000.

In August 1547 Somerset led an army into Scotland with Warwick, as has been said, as one of his subordinate commanders. They won the victory of Pinkie and, marching to the capital, occupied Leith. Haddington was made an English fortress. Mean-

while, an English rebellion was developing which would give
Dudley his true opportunity.

When Henry VIII died, the country districts had remained at
peace for more than ten years, since in fact the failure of the Pilgrimage of Grace which had so greatly disturbed both Yorkshire
and North Lincolnshire. Until 1569 the northern counties would
rest in peace. The memories of the executions were still quite
vivid; besides, that ill-judged venture had been a protest addressed
to a majestic sovereign, who was wrongly felt to be benevolent.
The North had no reason to place any hope in the intentions of the
Duke of Somerset.

The two risings which took place in the West Country and in
East Anglia were in fact hardly related to, and only the second
entered into, Lord Warwick's career. Throughout the whole
country the debasing of the currency had its effect. At the same
time, the steady growth of the wool market and the development
of cloth-making had their importance. The greater profits were to
be made from large-scale grazing. Thus Sir Robert Southwell at
this time was grazing almost ten thousand sheep on fourteen
different ranges, while the Spencers of Althorp ran flocks of thirteen thousand in the pasture county of Northamptonshire.[1]

The manufacture of woollens included such fabrics as broad-
cloths, kersies and friezes. The woollens were very heavy and
found their readiest markets in Northern and Eastern Europe. The
much finer worsteds were intended to compete for the Mediterranean and Iberian trade; but these were much less successful.
The kersies were manufactured in the West of England and the
broadcloth in the western Midlands and, above all, in Wiltshire.[2]

Somerset was interested in this trade and also in the ending of
enclosures. It may be said that the danger of revolt, whenever the
cause was economic, was always greater in those counties in which
the majority of men were relatively prosperous. It increased where
there were contacts with the capital, and where there was a certain knowledge of the trends of government. The Duke of Somerset
was known to have been concerned in certain bills aimed at improving the situation in the English countryside. The local feeling
against enclosures was always growing.

[1] Cf. *Edward VI: The Young King* by W. K. Jordan, pp. 402–9.   [2] *ibid*, pp. 404–5.

In May 1548 the Lord Protector had ordered the disparking of Hampton Park Chase which had been created by lands taken from eleven parishes in the last years of Henry VIII, when he waxed heavy with sickness and corpulence of body and could not go far to hunt.[1] The lands thus freed were ordered to be rented on the terms formerly prevailing. In the following year he caused an Act of Parliament to be passed, securing the protection of copy-holders on his own great estates, a matter which he could carry through since no one suffered except himself.

The actual rebellion, when it came, was quite unlike the northern risings. It was the only true rebellion of the agricultural population in which the local gentry took no part. Although it ended in actual conflict, it had indeed much of the character of a protest. It is sometimes suggested that its speedy development was due to the breakdown of the territorial power of the Dukes of Norfolk. This seems to me to be a misconception. There was in fact no Howard of the senior line left at liberty except a minor. The old Duke, now seventy-six years of age, was in the Tower of London, while the next heir, his grandson Thomas Howard, was a boy of thirteen living at Reigate under the guardianship of his aunt, the Duchess of Richmond, and receiving tuition along strictly Protestant lines from Edward Foxe, the martyrologist. But in any case, the Howard power was in a different region. The great houses of that stock were, with the exception of Mount Surrey, in the southern part of Norfolk and their affinity stretched southward across Suffolk to the Essex border. The area of protest lay to the north in inland Norfolk.

In this northern countryside the life of the gentry was well-developed and their houses, built of the East Anglian brick, were finer than those in the North of England. There was here no trace of feudalism in their relations with the yeomen and the peasantry. This was an area where for long there had been a sharp dislike between the agricultural workers and the possessing classes. There was also, on the part of the rebels, a determination to avoid the crime of arson, and the landlords had the prudence not to put their houses in a state of defence.

The actual rising occupied a quite restricted area, the disturb-

[1] *ibid*, p. 415.

ances began in Attleborough parish. It was a dull, in fact rather a dismal, countryside that lay along the road which separated Attleborough from Norwich, about thirteen miles away. The body of the rebels moved along the line now followed by the highway which runs north-eastward from Thetford to the county town.

The troubles first broke out on the night of 20 June 1549 and continued throughout the summer. The first act was the throwing down of hedges by small freeholders and copyholders engaged on corn farming. There was throughout a not very natural fear of the coming of sheep runs. The rebels feared old-fashioned dangers and also suggested some antique remedies.

The next episode just on a week later, involved Robert Kett, who held several farms in the neighbourhood of Wymondham. He not only agreed to take down his own hedges, but also offered himself as a leader. There was here a certain resemblance to the career of Robert Aske, who was caught up into the leadership of the Pilgrimage of Grace.

Robert Kett was a man of property verging on, but not yet amalgamated with, the landed gentry. His family, one branch of which was known as Knight, were locally well-known and very prosperous. He had five brothers, one of whom William, a butcher, joined and suffered with him. Curiously enough, among his property were three manors which he held as tenant of the Earl of Warwick. It seems to me that from the beginning Kett intended to negotiate; but he failed to realize that no man could ever negotiate with a Government when his supporters were in arms. He had a great reputation with the country people, a knowledge of their needs and of their aims.

The many differences between the rebels and the landed gentry included a sharp variation in their approach to organized religion. The nascent squirearchy and in particular the wealthier families were in constant contact with London and they contained a stiffening of courtiers. Their religious approach was in general still Henrican, and it was only later that it would hive off into the smallish Catholic minority and the main body of Anglican opinion, which would have its Puritan wing in the next generation.

The rebels are usually described as Protestant and this was certainly true of their leadership. It would, perhaps, be more

accurate to describe their outlook as radical. This would indicate
their opposition to the old-fashioned Conservatism, which marked
the standpoint of the North of England. In the urban districts
there was a positive Protestantism, the result of the contacts with
the men of the new faith who had come in from the Low Countries. It was in fact rather pathetic that the rebel chiefs seem to
have felt so strongly that bond of the new religion, which linked
them to the Lord Protector.

The groups of armed men converged almost inevitably upon
Norwich. The Bishop at that time was one of the least significant
in the long line of often distinguished men, who have held through
the centuries that great East Anglian diocese. William Rugg was
a Norfolk man of gentle birth, who had been the last Abbot of St
Benet's Hulme. He had been consecrated in the year following the
breach with Rome. He was not married and was in some respects
Conservative; but he was heavily in debt and before Christmas of
this same year he was compelled to resign his bishopric. He played
no part in Kett's rebellion.

Meanwhile, the rebel forces had reached Norwich and had
encamped at an elevated site slightly above the city at Mousehold
Heath. A stream of men came in to join them and also two considerable bodies, one from the neighbourhood of Castle Rising and
the other from the countryside round Yarmouth.

At Mousehold Heath Kett now established a well-disciplined
and Protestant community. He called upon the city's leaders to
help him to propose terms for a settlement, and in this he was
helped both by the mayor, Thomas Codd, and by Thomas Aldrich,
a wealthy merchant. Their position was quite safe, but Kett's was
dangerous. He was after all in command of a body of countrymen
under arms. By the end of July there were some ten thousand men
in camp with him.

The demands were in some respects quite curiously old-fashioned.
The men asked that lords of the manor should possess no rights in
common land and that meadow lands and marsh lands should be
as they were in I Henry VII, that is to say in 1485. They asked
for a standard bushel, that the keeping of dovecotes be strictly
limited, and that copyhold rents should be restored to those en-
forced in I Henry VII. They asked that the lords of the manor

E

should be prohibited from purchasing freehold lands and then
letting them out as copyholds. They denounced the sale of ward-
ships and the forced marriage of wards. They further asked that
no lord or gentleman be permitted to raise sheep and cattle, save
for the use of his own household.

There wasno doubt at all what the gentry of the county would
reply to these demands. There were also some religious elements.
It was demanded that incumbents who did not preach and 'set
forth the Word of God' should be put forth. There was never any
question of the acceptance of such proposals. The only question
was as to how the rebellion should be put down.

There are many aspects of the situation which are still obscure.
We cannot discern how the organization had arisen or how long the
idea of a revolt had been in preparation. It was characteristic of
the New Men to be intolerant of Papists. It does not seem to have
occurred to either of the Ketts to remember what had been the
consequences of the Pilgrimage of Grace. There was a curious
bone-headed energy in all the actions of Robert Kett.

The Duke of Somerset was in London, kept there by the still
continued smouldering of the antique-style rebellion, which had
broken out in the West Country. The other military leaders were
either in the western counties or on the Scottish borders, so Somerset placed the Marquess of Northampton in command. This was
the mistake of a leader who never really knew his close associates.
The Marquess was not only quite without military experience,
but he had no determination in his character. He went north and
entered Norwich on 30 July. The same night Kett attacked the
city in force. For two days there was hand-to-hand fighting and
then Northampton withdrew and returned to London. There
appeared to be only one way to save the country. The Lord Protector and the Council called upon the Earl of Warwick.

The possession of great riches made men cautious. It was not
the custom of the members of the Council to express their private
thoughts to the Duke of Somerset. It is likely that there were many
who foresaw that the protectorate would never be the same again
if victory should crown the arms of the Earl of Warwick.

This was the turning point of John Dudley's life. Henceforward
until the end he would be in actual or potential control of the

whole of England. One gains the impression that he knew well what this campaign would mean for him.

He acted with the greatest speed. Within a fortnight of receiving his instructions, he had assembled his forces at Cambridge. This was a campaign in which there was unanimity among the gentlemen of England. Their class required the immediate destruction of this rebellion. There was no hope for the unlettered men who stood under the rain on Mousehold Heath.

Lord Warwick had the gifts of leadership. He was always at his best in dealing with the younger officers of his own world. Like most great commanders he was wholly free from those intellectual interests which might separate him from the mass of his supporters. It was different with the tiny group of those young men who were the heirs to great possessions; but there was no need for him to enter into these pre-occupations now. He was going forward in the August weather to undertake the rule of England. His sons were all about him; he must have been content.

Beside the local levies and the gentlemen who had joined him, he had fifteen hundred mercenaries, for the most part Italians. His force numbered six thousand foot soldiers and fifteen hundred cavalry. They went from Cambridge across to Thetford and thence into Norwich along the road which Kett had followed. On 24 August the rebels had been driven out of the county town and fifty-nine of the captives were hanged in the market place. The camp on Mousehold Heath was isolated and its food supplies were very soon exhausted.

On 26 August Kett moved down into the valley. Warwick had gathered his gentlemen together. For many of them this victory would be their first experience of battle. They swore to conquer or to die; but there was in fact no danger of a disastrous outcome. The rebels were heavily defeated in Dussin's Dale. There was a local ballad which had forecast this misery: it gives a very clear impression of the situation:

> The country gnoffes hob, dick and hick
> With club and clooten shoon
> Shall fill the vale of Dussin's Dale
> With slaughtered bodies soon.

Kett fled and was soon captured. Robert Kett was hanged from the castle walls at Norwich, and his brother William from the church tower at Wymondham. This was before the end of that heavy summer. The Earl of Warwick was now in a position from which no rival could dislodge him.

III

Lord Seymour's End

As the Earl of Warwick rode southwards after his victory in Norfolk he must have seen that the situation was henceforward in his hands. He had brought his sons to a soldier's trade and the two eldest among the survivors had been with him in East Anglia. The eldest son, Sir Henry Dudley, had died in the town of Boulogne in 1545, a few weeks after he had been knighted for his actions in the taking of that fortress.

Warwick believed in arranging early marriages for his children. In the previous year Robert Dudley, then sixteen years of age, had been married to Amy, the only child of Sir John Robsart of Siderstern in Norfolk. She inherited a few manors from her father and her mother had brought in a London merchant's fortune. It was a perfectly suitable endowment for one of Warwick's younger sons. His second surviving son, Sir Ambrose Dudley, had been married, back in Henry VIII's reign, to the heiress of William Winwood, the attorney-general in those days. From the time of the Norfolk Rising his three elder sons would all be associated with his great career. The two youngest sons, Guildford and another Henry, were both still children.[1]

The Duke of Somerset's position was weak and growing weaker. There had been the long difficulties occasioned by his brother Thomas, Lord Seymour. Both brothers had owed their careers to their sister's marriage with King Henry; but beyond this they had very slender links. The younger brother was a fighter, who was attractive to women and unscrupulous where money was concerned. He had been Vice-Admiral in Henry VIII's reign and, as has been related, was made Lord High Admiral and a peer as

[1] There is a pedigree of his immediate family in British Museum, Stowe MSS, 6332.

Lord Seymour of Sudeley in the promotions which had been envisaged in King Henry's will. At the same time he had been made
a Knight of the Garter. From 1536 he had constantly built up his
landed property. At the beginning he had had nothing. It is hard
to form an exact impression; very little of his personal correspondence has survived.

When a young man he had sought the hand of Catherine Parr,
then Lady Latimer, but he had prudently retired when the King's
fancy had moved in that direction. It was therefore not unnatural
that he should have married her very soon after his sovereign's
death. In the following year she died and he had twice advanced
pretensions to the hand of Edward VI's stepsister, the Lady
Elizabeth. He also took Lady Jane Grey, the Marquess of
Dorset's eldest daughter into his household and formed a design to
marry her to his young master. The Duke would have preferred
that his own daughter Lady Jane Seymour should have made this
royal marriage, but she was only eight years old. The Duke of
Somerset would always over-estimate the time he had in which to
build his plans.

It is important not to overstress this project in the life and background of Jane Grey. She was only ten years of age when she was
sent, accompanied by her tutor John Aylmer whose influence will
be considered later, to dwell with Lord Seymour and his wife
Catherine the Queen Dowager. Here she found in flower through
the Queen's influence that Protestantism to which she had been
accustomed. There was also throughout the side of the women of
this household a Humanism, which she was not yet old enough to
understand.

Among those living with the Queen Dowager was the Lady
Elizabeth, Edward's sister. She had her own difficulties with the
Admiral, and at no time of her life does she seem to have had any
close relations with the Grey family.[1] At her christening the old
Marchioness of Dorset had held her at the font; but this was
merely one of those services which Henry VIII was accustomed to
require from his cousin's family. Curiously enough it was with the
Lady Mary and not the Lady Elizabeth that Lady Dorset maintained relations during this reign.

[1] For an excellent account of her early life cf. Alison Plowden, *The Young Elizabeth*.

At the same time it seems likely that Lady Jane's system of education can be traced first to the ideas of Catherine Parr and then to the elaborate methods used in the training of Lady Elizabeth. Catherine Parr appears to have developed her own intellectual interests in adult life. Although she was from an early stage very clearly Protestant in her sympathies, she belonged to the generation which still looked to Marguerite Queen of Navarre, whose Humanism always remained within the framework of a negligent Catholicism. It is worth remarking that one of the earliest of the Lady Elizabeth's literary efforts was the presentation to Queen Catherine of Marguerite's long poem which was known in English by the title of *The Mirror of the Sinful Soul*.

It was during Lady Jane's stay with the Queen Dowager that William Grindal, a Fellow of St John's College, Cambridge and the tutor to Lady Elizabeth in her Greek studies, died of the Plague and was succeeded by Roger Ascham, who had recommended him. Ascham would re-appear in a later stage of Lady Jane Grey's education. Indeed others of the Queen Dowager's circle, notably Sir John Cheke and Sir Anthony Cooke, would re-appear in the course of her brief career.

Roger Ascham was at this time thirty-three years of age, coming from an established Yorkshire family of the middle rank then settled at Kirby Wiske outside Northallerton. His father was domestic steward to Lord Scrope of Bolton. Roger had been received as a child into the household of Sir Anthony Wingfield, who had sent him at his expense to St John's College, Cambridge. He was an English example of the Erasmian scholar whose learning was his stock-in-trade. He had, however, a fashionable interest in sport and had composed a well-known treatise on archery. He had been from his early years a Protestant, but he was uninterested in the world of politics. He brought his learning to all kinds of patrons. John Aylmer was also a Cambridge man, though from Queen's College.

Ascham used with the Lady Elizabeth the method of a double translation in teaching both Latin and Greek. Thus she read almost the whole of Cicero and a great part of Livy re-translating the passages back into Latin again. The same method was employed in their Greek studies using Demosthenes and the Greek New Testament. Ascham also concentrated upon penmanship; in the case of Lady Elizabeth he is even seen mending her silver pen. It seems rather strange that even in England there should be so much stress after French upon Italian. This may be seen as the still continuing consequence of the Italian origins of the earlier Humanism.

It does not seem that at this period German was among the languages that was studied. All the correspondence both with the German princes and with the leaders of the Reformed Churches in Germany seems to have been carried on in Latin.

At the same time it seems clear that these linguistic studies were purely exercises. None of these learned ladies, neither Queen Catherine nor the Lady Elizabeth nor the Lady Jane, had ever passed beyond the shores of England. No detailed scheme of the historical knowledge of the distant past seems ever to have been conveyed to them. The speeches of Cicero as an example conveyed a knowledge of Latin, but not an understanding of Roman history. If this should in fact have been the case it suggests a rather arid form of knowledge. But there was one factor that was conveyed in certain cases and in particular in that of Lady Jane and this was a burning religious faith. Whatever else she learned during her girlhood from her contemporaries and also from the members of her own family there was one thing that was peculiarly her own and that was a clear and quite unbreakable attachment to the new religion.

Apart from the long-term consequences of Ascham's influence on John Aylmer, the effect on Lady Jane of this stay with Queen Catherine was transient. Lord Seymour's establishment was moved to his new estate of Sudeley in Gloucestershire and there Catherine Parr died suddenly on 5 September 1548 losing at the same time her new-born child. She was buried at Sudeley in the chapel there with all the ceremonies that were owing to a widow of King Henry. Lady Jane Grey was the young chief mourner.

It would seem that with Queen Catherine's death the significance of this episode in Lady Jane's childhood was concluded. Lady Elizabeth had already moved to Sir Anthony and Lady Denny's house at Cheshunt. When Lord Seymour fell Lady Jane returned to her own parents. It is not suggested that she was ever an important factor in Lord Seymour's life. She was merely the subject of one of his many plans which had miscarried.

Lord Seymour's small eyes looked out over his bushy beard. The disobliged Protestant noblemen were rare; there were very few beside Lord Dorset. The usual description of Lord Seymour's character is, perhaps, over-simplified. He is seen as a simple fellow, a common rogue. This was a type that was to recur in the history of great landed families in later generations; it was known as the 'black sheep'. His brother with his high-minded outlook would certainly have a natural antipathy for such a man. The Duke was well-contented with his own work. It is worth re-marking that in the Victorian period it was seldom recognized how the satisfaction of a Calvinist belief united to the possession of worldly riches could arouse antagonism. In France the case of Gaspard de Coligny was an exact parallel.

There was much that was hard to understand in Somerset's character. It seems that he felt that he could build up a great ducal house and, strangely enough, that there was ample time for this. It never appears that he foresaw Lord Warwick as a rival until his disaster was about to overtake him. He was in some ways a solitary figure. His wife joined with him in his practices of piety, for the rest she was proud and overbearing and her temperament was alive with jealousy. She was also most extravagant. Her stores of robes and jewellery would in the end be confiscated and later used to deck out Jane Grey and her relations.

Somerset had a great capacity for amassing wealth, apparently almost unconsciously. It was not so much the lands of the chantries which he suppressed as the way in which, as Lord Protector, properties could come to him. His work of constructing his great seats was meticulous and very leisurely. The long range of Somer-set House along the river recalls the site of his large London resi-dence, and deep in the Savernake Forest he was laying out that country palace which he did not live to build.

Somerset was in certain ways a complex personality. His reli-gion made him certainly high-minded. On the other hand his character was much more ordinary; it was seamed with greed. He was by nature solemn and also rather secretive. It was this fact of his great possessions which had its effect upon the outlook of John

Dudley, who combined, like Wallenstein, a great military capacity with a desire for landed wealth.

The difficulties created by Lord Seymour's way of life were soon apparent. He had close contacts with those outside the law, which members of his class in general avoided. When he was Lord Admiral, it seems that he had relations with the pirate Thomasson, whom he left in peace in the Scilly Islands, and he obtained through Sir William Sharington control of the mint at Bristol. He early discovered that Sir William had misused his office as vice-treasurer by illegally coining testoons or shilling pieces, and became his partner. He intended to use these false coins to increase the purchase of the arms that he was assembling secretly at Holt Castle in North Wales. Somerset's trouble with his brother masked for him the dangers of his situation.

It is not surprising that the more orthodox members of the Government demanded Lord Seymour's destruction. At the same time, it cannot be said that he presented a real peril to the Lord Protector for no one would have cast him down to replace him by another member of his own family. Seymour was imprisoned in the Tower of London on 17 January 1549. It would have been prudent to have kept him there for life. That the Houses of Parliament should have consented to his condemnation was only natural; but it was a great mistake for the Lord Protector to agree to his brother's execution, which took place on 20 March. This opened the way for his own journey to the block. The Duke of Somerset, who spent so much time in perusing the Good Book, should have given more thought to the narrative of Cain and Abel.

When Warwick came back to London, the Protestant Reformation had already been established. He had never been associated with the great episcopal figures of the reign's beginning, Gardiner, Bonner, and Tunstall. The attempt that they had made to retain the ecclesiastical structure of King Henry's reign had come to failure. By this time Bishops Gardiner and Bonner were in the Tower; when Warwick came to power he would retain them there.

At the same time it may be suggested that he was without any feeling for that Messianic attachment to the Old Testament which held together all the various adepts of the new religion. This was

the faith that united the Duke of Somerset with Edward Underhill, the Hot Gospeller, and with all those artisans in London and
in East Anglia, who were unaccustomed to the printed word and
who would sit over the Old Testament with its heavy type, pick-
ing out slowly and with attention the attractive stories which were
there set out so logically. There was no place at the Earl of
Warwick's table for the Hot Gospeller. Few men were ever more
remote than Warwick was from the spring-time of the new religion.

It was motives of quite a different character that kept John
Dudley faithful to Henry VIII's religious settlement, as this became slowly clear. The break-up of the ancient Church had handed
over vast estates to the disposition of the Crown. First of all there
had been the possessions of all the monasteries in England and
now the lesser matter of the chantry lands. In the immediate
future there would be the paring down of the landed properties of
the English bishoprics. It was only the adherents of the New Religion, or to speak more exactly their worldly leaders, who were in a
position to acquire these rich estates.

Leaving aside the high talents with which he was endowed,
John Dudley remained all his life what he had been brought up to
be, an Henrican courtier. Two duties remained always paramount,
to serve the King and to look after himself. There was in consequence a certain simplicity about his actions. His military qualities
brought about his rise to power.

IV

The Young King

The character of the young King formed early and he always seems to have been aware that he was the son and heir of a great sovereign. Edward VI had been nine years of age at his accession. He was armoured by an intense religious belief which must itself have served to build up his unusual isolation. Affection was not strong in him and he seems to have had none for the Princesses Mary and Elizabeth. He seems never to have liked the Seymour family. On the one hand they were too close to him and on the other they had no share in what he really prized, his royal blood.

He was soon used to praise from humanists and churchmen. Nicholas Ridley, Bishop of Rochester, preached regularly before him and he had an especial taste for the sermons of Dr Latimer. The sons of the ruling clique were all about him; Lord Hertford, who was Somerset's heir and Lord Lisle, who was Warwick's and Lord Maltravers. who was Arundel's. One can sense that there was no intimacy here. Two of his companions ended up as Catholics, Lord Giles Paulet and Lord Lumley. His tutors were Dr Richard Coxe, Sir Anthony Cooke and Sir John Cheke; for Cheke he showed an affection. It seems that the only one of his companions whom he really liked was a young Irishman, Barnaby Fitzpatrick, later Lord Upper Ossory.[1]

Edward was not fond of sport and did not travel. In early youth his health was good. His life was wholly passed in the Home Counties. He was slim and rather short with steady grey eyes; he dressed with considerable splendour. He was both proud and wary, and one seems to sense, a trifle humourless.

When he was quite young, it was proposed that King Edward

---

[1] Cf. *Correspondence with Lord Upper Ossory* printed by Horace Walpole, 1772.

should marry the Queen of Scots; but she eluded him. An engagement was afterwards suggested with the eldest daughter of the King of France. It seems that the disparity in religions would in fact have made this impracticable, and nothing came of it. She was the most beautiful of the Valois Princesses and later became the Queen of Spain.

The Chronicle of King Edward VI, which was edited by Professor W. K. Jordan in 1966, is a first-hand document of real importance. The editor's suggestion that the entries made between 1 July 1550 and the last note, which is dated 30 November 1552, were all made at the time by the young sovereign appears convincing.[1] On this assumption the King was just thirteen years of age when he began his record.

The entries are all in his own handwriting, but in certain instances, such as the details of the Calais fortification and the list of various types of gun, it seems likely that they were copied from official papers. They therefore do not necessarily convey the extent of the King's knowledge.

He had no experience of foreign travel and his understanding of the French language has perhaps been exaggerated. Curiously, he appears to have had some detailed information as to the relationships of the members of the House of Guise-Lorraine, an unlikely subject. As an example he gives the second Duke of Guise the title of Marquis of Mayenne, which he held for a period in his father's lifetime.[2] The fact that Edward spells Ambleteuse as Hamleteu and accepts the latter form as a French name must give one pause.[3]

At the same time Henry II, King of France, was the only sovereign with whom he was in contact. Edward VI appears to have taken his future marriage with the Princess of France quite seriously and seems to have looked upon Henry II as his prospective father-in-law. The boy was much pleased by the Order of St Michel, which Henry sent to him, and he notes that at Michaelmas he wore its *insignia*. He expressed pleasure at the coming of the Maréchal de St André, the special ambassador. 'I answered the envoy that I thanked him (the French King) for his Order and

[1] *The Chronicles and Political Papers of King Edward VI*, introduction, pp. xvii–xviii.
[2] *ibid*, p. 24.   [3] *ibid*, p. 150.

also for his love, and that I would show love at all points.'[1] He
agreed to be Godfather to the King's third son, the Duc d'Angoulême, who was christened Edward Alexander and lived to
reign in France as Henry III.[2] Although religion is not mentioned
in these French contacts, it is worth noting that the link was not
Calvinism, for even those great French leaders who adopted the
Reformed Religion did not make this change in Edward's lifetime.

Apart from these contacts, Edward's contact with foreigners
was for the most part confined to exiled theologians. Among these
the man who made the greatest impression on him was Martin
Bucer. He was at this time nearing sixty years of age, by birth a
citizen of Schlettstadt in Alsace, then a Dominican and now, for
some twenty years, a minister at Strasbourg of Zwinglian opinions.
He came to settle in England in 1549 and died some eighteen
months later. The entry in the *Chronicle* is full of interest. 'The
learned man Bucer,' wrote Edward, 'died at Cambridge, who was
two days afterward buried in St Mary's Church at Cambridge,
all the whole university with the whole town bringing him to the
grave to the number of 3,000 persons; also there was an oration of
Mr Haddon made very eloquently at his death and a sermon of
[Dr Matthew Parker]. After that Mr Redman made a third sermon. Which three sermons made the people wonderfully to lament
his death.'[3] This gives a clear indication of the King's thought. A
sermon had a real appeal to the young sovereign in his earnest
piety. In this he differed from many of those who were his councillors.

Another comment will build up the picture.[4] 'A certain Arian
of the strangers, a Dutchman [this was in fact George van Parris],
being excommunicated by the congregation of his countrymen,
was after long disputation condemned to the fire.' An overt piety
based on an ineradicable spiritual self-confidence is not likely to
make a lad popular. The King was a lonely boy.

The King's exact information was confined to the road southwards to Paris and to those eastern avenues which led through the
Low Countries and to the towns, which lay along them. Beyond

---

[1] *ibid*, p. 72.
[2] So described *ibid*, p. 101, but it really should be Duc d'Anjou.
[3] *ibid*, pp. 54-5.   [4] *ibid*, p. 58.

this region his knowledge faltered. There were references to the State entry into Rouen made by Henry II and to the meeting of the English envoy with the Duke of Montpensier at Château-briant.[1]

He mentions the then German cities of Strasbourg and Augsburg, which he calls by their Latin names, Argenta and Augusta. He had a boy's interest in battles and there are three references to Andrea Doria's attack on the city of Africa.[2] There is a comment on Gustavus, King of the East Land and one reference each to the Prince of Denmark and the Prince of Portugal, *prétendants* for the hand of his half-sister, the Lady Mary. Otherwise there are no comments as to persons or to places in the Iberian Peninsula or in the lands under the Northern Crowns. Leaving aside the multitude of French nobility, he mentions George, Duke of Mecklenburg and his three earls, the Rhinegrave,[3] the Duke of Parma, and the Prince of Macedonia. The whole diary is therefore starred with titles. It does not seem that they meant much to him.

Many of these references are trivial, but this does not apply to what King Edward wrote about his councillors. The rather frequent comments on the Earl of Warwick seem to express a fear, a not unnatural emotion in the young boy. It is possible this may be fanciful. Edward VI had always admired his royal father and the late sovereign had in the course of time removed his highest officers. At any rate, as a general rule, the young King was cold at heart towards his councillors.

[1] *ibid*, p. 66. The reference here is to Châteaubriant and the entry contains the phrase 'booted and spurred', almost the first use of this expression.
[2] Cf. *ibid*, pp. 42, 45 and 47. These entries all refer to the attack on Mehedia.
[3] Philip Francis of Bavaria.

V

Somerset's Fall

The fall of the Protector Somerset was essentially in the nature of a military operation. The position can be described quite simply. There were four areas in which troops were placed. There were those on the northern border against the Scots and then the two bodies used for putting down the two rebellions. There was also a small force of merely five hundred men kept by the Duke of Somerset to guard the King.

In London there were the soldiers whom the Earl of Warwick had brought down from his successful operations in East Anglia and about Salisbury there were the troops which had been used in the West Country under Lord Russell. With Russell there was the force which Lord Herbert could raise from his headquarters at Wilton.

Somerset was at Hampton Court and for the moment he had with him the King. With him was Paget, his now disregarded mentor, and the Archbishop of Canterbury. What support could the Protector expect from this high prelate? Cranmer must have sympathized to some extent with Somerset for he was closer to him than to any other leader; but it cannot be said of him that he was of assistance in a struggle which turned upon the military control. It must also be mentioned that he was too close to the centre of affairs to imagine that any other practicable government would be less pledged to Reformation principles.

Cranmer had long experience of mundane power and was full of knowledge, but not perspicacious. There was that in his high Regalian temper which led him to be cossetted by men whom he did not fully understand. The late King had always prized him. His enemies in the episcopate had been brought down. Ever since

1 Edward VI. Artist unknown, based on a drawing
of 1543 after Holbein.

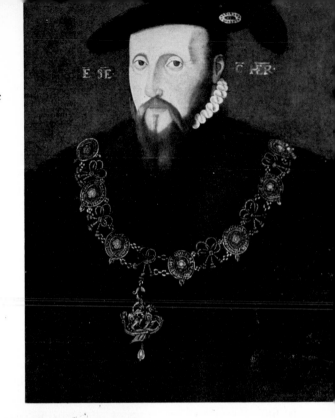

2 The Duke of Somerset, one of the only two surviving portraits.

3 Sir William Paget, the portrait attributed to the Master of the Stätthalterin Madonna.

he had been elevated to the primacy his life was very smooth for him. The young sovereign, his godson, had a certain reverence for his beliefs; perhaps he put more trust than he should have done in the King's piety.

There was a certain kindness in Cranmer's temperament which, combined with his own high place, made his equals treat him with respect. He was also the *fulcrum* of the exiles, the name which brought the foreign Protestants to cross the Channel. On a personal level he surely derived much satisfaction from the lovely prose with which he was endowing the Church of England. The admirable portrait by Gerlach Flicke painted in 1552 shows him a compact figure with grey eyes and brown hair flecked with white, wearing a rochet and a grey chimere, lined with black and a stole of brown fur above black satin.[1] The chair in which he sits is decorated with elaborate inlaid work and upholstered in scarlet, with fringing of red and green. Behind him is a diamond-paned window opening on to a calm blue sky. He is seen thus at the summit of his prosperity in the last contented period of his tranquil life.

During Henry VIII's reign he had had to tack and tack and he must have found that sovereign's Conservatism wearing; but now that he was free the old doctrines slipped away from him. He could see those Protestant values, which were so close to his heart, make steady headway like a flowing tide.

To the Earl of Warwick, the Archbishop did not present a problem. Dudley had determined, as has been indicated, to support the Reformation Settlement. In consequence he would maintain the King's archbishop. It was always his determination to avoid unnecessary trouble. There was not much in common between the characters of Cranmer and the Earl of Warwick. Dudley's preference among the divines of the New Religion was for men of a more freebooting type. Cranmer stood apart from all those circumstances which led to the removal of the Duke of Somerset.

It may be said that neither the popular Protantism of London, nor the Roman Catholic enclaves throughout the country had any effect on the change of government which was now effected. The legend of a Catholic support for the Earl of Warwick, which

---

[1] This portrait now hangs in the National Portrait Gallery.

has been so long established and is still brought forward by Professor Jordan,[1] can no longer be maintained. It turns upon the practice of attributing a secret Catholic purpose to the Earls of Southampton and Arundel. Southampton has been shown by Dr A. L. Rowse[2] to have made about this time a will that was explicitly Protestant and there is no reason to suppose that the latter had any interest in re-constituting the old religion.[3]

The artisan section of the London population, what can be called roughly the upper working class, held for the most part a strongly Evangelical religion, which had seeped in from the Low Countries during the last twenty years. It was bound up with the fact that this section was separated from the country folk, and from the London proletariat, by being newly literate. A single instance will illuminate this situation. At the parish church of St Martin in Ironmongers' Lane, the clergyman and churchwardens had taken down the crucifix and statues and placed the royal arms where the crucifix had stood. They had adorned the walls with texts from Scripture. The effect of the plain whitewash and the new wording painted dark upon it was very striking. It taught those who could now read for the first time that they did well to meditate on the Word of God. These texts all came from the Testaments and could be spelled out and digested. Their readers' knowledge of history was rudimentary and foreshortened. Their God was near to them and spoke in terms that there was no mistaking. This was attractive to all those who, like Edward VI and Cranmer, followed the New Teaching. At the same time, these artisans had little military significance. To the Earl of Warwick this all meant nothing. His whole thought was bound up with the kingdoms of this world.

The problem which faced Warwick was relatively simple and he proceeded to tackle it with sober caution. He wished to remove the Lord Protector from his office. The victim would, however, according to this plan, receive his liberty and would remain about the Court. The Council would appoint a committee to exercise the powers that he had held. Inevitably there would be rewards.

---

[1] Jordan, *op. cit.*, p. 91.
[2] A. L. Rowse, *Shakespeare's Southampton, Patron of Virginia*, p. 24.
[3] Cf. This work, pp. oo-o.

The arrangements were carried out with perfect smoothness. The Lord Protector had united all the landowners against him; he had acted against the privileges of their class. He had attacked their rights to maintain enclosures. There was no one among the rich who would support him on this issue.

There were of course some who had personal cause of complaint against him. Thus Lord Northampton blamed him for his failure to terminate his marriage with Lady Anne Bourchier, the only child of the last Earl of Essex of that family whose great estates he had obtained.[1]

The first necessity for the Earl of Warwick was to engage the support of Lord Herbert and Lord Russell and, in consequence, to neutralize the forces that they had under their command. The task was easy and they were both promised promotions in the peerage; they received, respectively, the earldoms of Pembroke and Bedford. But most of the great men had no soldiers; their consent could therefore be presumed.

Meanwhile the rest of the Council had been gathering in London, where Warwick held meetings with them at Ely House. It was for all these reasons a simple matter for Lord Warwick to convince them. The only soldiers in the City were those whom he had himself brought back from Norfolk. He decided that they should occupy the Tower of London. The Duke of Somerset at Windsor had none of the leaders with him except Archbishop Cranmer. Among minor characters, Paget was also with him. On the question of a policy for agriculture Paget agreed with all his class, but he had, from the beginning of the reign, been the âme damnée of the Protector. The Council, urged by Warwick, made its move; for his part the Archbishop would not oppose them.

As he was fresh to his great power, Warwick acted very cautiously. Once the Lord Protector had consented to lay down his office, he was conducted to the Tower of London by the Earls of Huntingdon and Southampton. This was Southampton's last public action and he soon vanishes from the scene. The Duke of

[1] She had fled from him as long ago as 1543, when she was sixteen years of age and he was anxious to regularize the relationship that he had formed with Lord Cobham's daughter. In these years between the legal ending of the nullity arrangements of the Church of Rome and the establishment of divorce by private Act of Parliament the situation was often tricky.

Somerset did not stay there long. After a certain paring down of his great properties, he was released and returned to Court; a place was reserved for him on the Privy Council. He and his children were after all the nearest relatives of the young sovereign. Further, a marriage was arranged, which took place in the King's presence, between the Duke's daughter, Lady Anne and Lord Lisle, who was the Earl of Warwick's eldest son. Few changes in that agitated century had taken place so very tranquilly.

VI

Northumberland's Power

Once the Duke of Somerset had been removed from the seat of power, the Earl of Warwick built up very quickly his great position. A mere recital will serve to indicate how very complete was his control. He took over once more, but this time only for a few months, his former post of Lord High Admiral. He also obtained, as a life appointment, the post of Governor of Northumberland, with which he combined that of Warden of the Marches towards Scotland, so much for his military power.

He also took the precaution of receiving the chief stewardship of the late palatinate of Durham. On the governorship and on this new office, he soon would hinge the basis of his landed influence. He also decided to accept the office of joint commissioner and overseer of the Mint. It was important that the Court itself should be within his immediate control and he became Lord Steward of the Household and also, Earl Marshal. With a view to the control of politics, he undertook the office of Lord President of the Council. It was important that no key posts should be left within the power of rivals.

He had an evident desire to rule by fear; he was not a man of whom his equals could ask a favour. As far as rewards went, apart from the two earldoms offered in return for the control of the soldiers in the West, he was not inclined to raise up any man who could in time be a competitor. Lord Treasurer Paulet had a claim for he had joined with Warwick in entertaining the members of the Council. He was a careful, prudent politician with an orderly mind and a nice judgment; he always knew which way the wind was blowing. He thus became the Marquess of Winchester. The two young Dukes of Suffolk had both died recently and that dukedom was conferred on the Marquess of Dorset. He was a God-send to the new ruler, a quiet and timorous man, about whose judgment Warwick never had to trouble. Beyond this there were no more rewards. On 11 October 1551, the Earl of Warwick accepted from the King the dukedom of Northumberland.

One of his problems was how he should deal with the Lady Mary. By her father's will she had been left as heiress-presumptive to the Crown. She received, so long as she remained unmarried, an annuity of £3,000, chiefly drawn from her manors of Newhall and Hunsdon in the Home Counties and Kenninghall in East Anglia.

Her position in the religious difficulties in which she was involved was stronger than is sometimes realized. Her constant claim was to preserve the Mass, which her father had left to the nation. She had accepted the oath of supremacy in his reign and from this she never veered, until she came to her own accession. Throughout the period of her brother's rule, she made no references to the Pope. No one interfered with the way in which she ruled her house, as long as the Duke of Somerset remained in power.

At the same time it was the Mass, whether Roman or Henrican, to which the young King was opposed and Northumberland was readier than his predecessor had been to yield to his sovereign's wishes. Edward VI had meditated long on the Good Book and there could discern the marvellous ways in which the Roman idolatries had been foreshadowed. The Emperor Charles V had made a somewhat imprudent intervention on his niece's behalf. When the Council suggested to the sovereign that he might permit his sister to continue in her disobedience in order to pacify the foreign powers, his reply was unequivocal.

'Are these things so, My Lords,' exclaimed King Edward, 'is it lawful by Scripture to sanction idolatry?'

'There were good Kings in Scripture,' answered his councillors, 'who allowed the hill altars and yet were called good.'[1]

The sovereign's reply was quite in character. 'We follow the example of good men, when they have done well. We do not follow them in evil. David was good, but David seduced Bath-

---

[1] This vivid exchange is printed in Froude, *History*, iv, pp. 567–8.

shebah and murdered Uriah. We are not to imitate David in such deeds as these. Is there no better Scripture?'

Such exchanges must have been hard to deal with for those brought up at King Henry's Court. As for Northumberland, it would seem that he never interfered with his young sovereign in this narrow field. It was probably an act of prudence not to disturb the King in his true interests.

As a consequence, a body of Councillors was sent down to investigate the Lady Mary's household. Her principal chaplain, Francis Mallett, who had approached her on the side of her humanist interests, was removed from her house for celebrating Mass. It is an example of the confusion of the time that Dr Mallett was a strong Henrican, a *protégé* of both Cromwell and Cranmer, who died eventually as an Anglican and Dean of Lincoln.

It is evident that the past weighed heavily on the Lady Mary. Her closest friend, the Marchioness of Exeter, remained a prisoner in the Tower throughout this reign. She did not encourage visits, especially from those who might conceivably be thought of as disaffected.[1] In fact, so long as she did not approach the Pope and remained aloof from the internal politics of England, the Lady Mary was quite safe. As far as the Dukes of Somerset and Northumberland were concerned, it seems that she had no temptation to distinguish between these cormorants.

Northumberland had decided to keep aside the old great families. It was this, perhaps, which brought the Earl of Arundel into opposition. It is really strange that any man could seriously have hoped to overturn Northumberland. The Duchess of Somerset's anger was more understandable. She felt her exclusion from all power most keenly and brought her brother Sir Michael Stanhope, and also Sir Thomas Arundell, into her plans. There was an attempt to secure some help from Paget. This is surprising for, in order to neutralize his opposition, he had recently received a peerage as Lord Paget of Beaudesert.

Thomas Palmer, a soldier of fortune who had for long been associated with the minor military appointments about the Court,

[1] Her principal ecclesiastical adviser was John Hopton, a former Dominican and Prior of the Oxford Blackfriars, who had become her confessor when he was rector of the parish of St Agnes and St Anne, in the city of London.

revealed these stirrings to Northumberland. He received a knight-hood and became one of the new leaders' captains until the end. He was the last man whom Somerset should have thought of trust-ing, but the former Lord Protector never failed to show a lack of judgment.

This was the test for the new Duke's policy. He could hardly allow Somerset to survive once he had become a centre of dis-affection. Quietness was of course a great deal to ask for from the Lord Protector, since this would mean not only a complete absten-tion from the field of politics, but also the abandonment of a way of life which he was only now fashioning, the end of all his building plans for Somerset House and also for his country palace at Savernake.

At the same time Northumberland displayed a repugnance for shedding his equals' blood. His desire for power was bound up with the need to preserve peace among the great men of the realm. If he killed Arundel he might have a blood feud. For this reason there were no deaths from this nascent conspiracy, except for the Duke of Somerset and three men of lesser rank, Sir Michael Stan-hope, Sir Thomas Arundell, and Sir Ralph Vane.

In his journal the young King recites the charges against Somerset, including his determination to kill Northumberland. There is no real evidence that this was his intention. The Duchess of Somerset was sent to the Tower, where she joined the distin-guished prisoners already there, the old Duke of Norfolk and the Bishops of Winchester and London, Gardiner and Bonner. They were well treated in confinement and all survived to be released eventually at the accession of Queen Mary. Edward VI was cold towards his former guardian. On 22 January 1552 he made this note.[1] 'The Duke of Somerset had his head cut off upon Tower Hill between eight and nine o'clock in the morning.'

[1] *Chronicle*, p. 107.

I

The Rise of Cecil

The Duke of Northumberland began his period of rule in making a most excellent choice among his public servants. He chose Sir William Cecil as his adviser and it was his great misfortune that he made no use of his advice. Even as a young man, the great Lord Burghley was wonderfully suited to be a royal servant. He had early become a Protestant and his two marriages, the first short-lived union with Mary Cheke and the second with Mildred, daughter of Sir Anthony Cooke of Gidea Park in Essex, had brought him into the centre of the world of the wealthy, academic, Protestant humanists. His brother-in-law by his first marriage, Sir John Cheke, was later his colleague at Court. Cecil was himself a man of independent wealth and was in no sense a client of any of the great families. In 1552 he inherited an ample estate upon his father's death, which brought him the manor house of Burghley and lands in Rutland and Northamptonshire. He received in inheritance some small Court offices, the post of bailiff of Wittlesea Mere and that of the keeper of the swans in the fen country. By this time he had already received several manors, Barchamstow and Deeping in Lincolnshire, the manor and hall of Thetford in that county, and Liddington in Rutland. This was a substantial background for a young man who had only entered St John's College, Cambridge, in 1535.

He also had begun to acquire lands in the South of England, the rectory and manor of Wimbledon, where he could take the purer air. His town house was at Cannon Row in Westminster and he had thirty-six servants who wore his badge and livery.

Although he had few connexions with the great world, there were two exceptions, in each case the family was linked with his roots in Lincolnshire. These were Katharine, Duchess of Suffolk, and Lord Clinton; the Duchess was staunchly Protestant. This was his position when the Duke gave him the office of Secretary of State. There seems no evidence that at any time of his life was he interested in sport. Gout came to him early and he is described as riding round his garden on a small mule. He was 'rather meanly-statured', his hair and beard were brown. He was deeply interested in his own pedigree and, in general, was concerned with genealogy. Throughout his life he would scribble fragments of such detail on the backs of letters. It says much for Northumberland's breadth of view that he favoured such a character.

William Cecil had begun in the personal service of the Duke of Somerset, being his secretary and master of requests, in effect he ran his private office. When Somerset's first fall was impending, he saw that his ruin was inevitable and transferred his services to the new master. It was accepted as a custom of that age to make such changes.

Some of his aphorisms are worth recording; they give a clear impression of his whole outlook. 'That gentleman who sells an acre of land sells an ounce of credit, for gentility is nothing else but ancient riches. Beware of being surety for thy best friends; he that payeth another man's debts ensureth his own decay.' There is another phrase which comes from a later time. 'Suffer not thy sons to cross the Alps.'

A letter which Northumberland sent to him gives a pleasant impression of their personal relations. It was written just before his father's death. 'And', wrote Northumberland, 'for your gentle and most friendly request to have me at your father's on my way northwards, I do ever so semblably render my hearty thanks unto you, assuring you I will not omit to see him as I go by him, though I do but drink a cup of wine with him at the door, for I will not trouble no friend's house of mine otherwise on this journey, my train is so great and will be, whether I will or not. And for your being there, as I think myself much behelden to you that will take such pains; and to be a singular pleasure to have so much of your company; so could I rejoice for your own health that you might have such a *cantell* of recreation.'[1]

[1] S.P.Dom,Edward VI, XIV, 34 dated 31 May 1552.

The key to one aspect of Cecil's character was that he possessed an honest veneration for the territorial aristocracy. He had never travelled and even when he was quite young, he wished for splendour. To see what he achieved it is only necessary to look at Burghley House in the parish of Stamford St Martin, in the Soke of Peterborough. It is a vast work of pure splendour unmarred by taste. He gave his life to it; he was an uncommunicative man.

He lived in a period which was sunny for the class he wished to join. The law was kept and crime was punished, the rich grew richer. Had these opening stages of his life been more propitious for him, he would then have made a great Secretary of State. It is strange that Sir William Cecil, who was destined to such years and years of power, appears from the start of his career always as a great man in chrysalis. It is this that separates him from his contemporaries in the Secretariate of State, from Sir William Petre and Sir John Cheke. He saw dispassionately and from below the main contestants, the rich peers without armed forces and the Duke of Northumberland and his troops. His life and his experience were perfectly civilian; he had a clear understanding of what a politician could achieve with his own soldiers. He had a deep devotion to the Laws of England. There is little doubt as to what answer he would have given to Northumberland had he set before him his crucial problem.

Sir William Cecil was only a spectator throughout the period of the development of the catastrophe. Among Englishmen he had perhaps the deepest influence in the material development of his great country. He had long views and a steady insight. We can imagine him as he rode on his little mule in Wimbledon in the pure air.

II

The Old Religion

There is no period since the breach with Rome in which it is more difficult to assess the number of supporters of, and indeed the nature of support for, the old religion in England than in the six years of the reign of Edward VI. There was no regular penal legislation and much of our knowledge comes from disparate fragments of information. One point can be asserted with a certain confidence; there was almost no support for the old faith in the actual circles of the Government itself.

In one region the situation was quite different. In great areas across the whole of the North Country, there remained among the people of the countryside a deep attachment to all the aspects of the old religion. They had nothing but regret for their separation from the great body of Catholic Christendom. It was still quite recently, only in the spring and summer of 1537, that the Yorkshire villages had been marked by the hanging corpses of those who had taken part in the Pilgrimage of Grace. Admittedly that rebellion was kept to the eastern side of the Pennines; but the western shores of the north country were still more remote from any power of the London government. It was also very far from any real episcopal influence. The parishes to the southward of the Ribble were subject to the diocese of Lichfield far away in the midland counties. There was in western Lancashire nothing resembling the effect of Protestant propaganda. The greatest landowner, the Earl of Derby, was in religious matters roughly a Conservative and his wife (*née* Margaret Barlow) remained a strict Catholic. In the wild country around Ribblesdale the estates were large but of small value. The adjoining properties of Sir John Southworth of Samlesbury and his cousin, Thomas Hoghton of

Hoghton Tower, both of them Catholics, extended to over thirty thousand acres. There is also no reason to suppose that the farmers in the Fylde and their tenants were in the least affected by the changes in London.

The parish priests were for the most part local men, the sons of the neighbouring farmers, helped out by the surviving monks who had been turned out of their houses when the monasteries had been suppressed. Lord Derby was in London from time to time; but there is no evidence that Lord Cumberland ever went there. The rural squires and, above all, the farmers lived all their lives in their home counties.

Here in Lancashire, even York was far away. There was a northern independence among both the clergy and their flocks. The idea of the King made no appeal and men had hardly heard of Seymour and Dudley.

The situation was very different in the Midlands and in the South of England, where one could never be unconscious of the actions and the changing views of Government. There the active Catholics were always conscious that they were members of a fairly small minority. The comment made many years later by Cecily Lady Stonor brings out this point. In 1581 she was arrested on a charge of harbouring Father Campion. When called before the justices she made this statement.[1] 'I was born in such a time when holy mass was in great reverence, and was brought up in the same faith. In King Edward's time this reverence was neglected and reproved by such as governed. In Queen Mary's time it was restored with much applause.' She was at this time an old lady and had been married to Sir Francis Stonor in 1552; she was the daughter of Sir Leonard Chamberlayne of Shirburn Castle and a niece of Sebastian Newdigate, one of the Carthusians killed in 1537. It was not difficult for a family of the squirearchy to carry forward with its own beliefs, provided that it avoided any contact with the Government.

The Catholic body in the South of England went forward in general without cohesion. In some cases they belonged to the older generation of the wealthy landowners, men now remote from the Court, the inheritors of estates in the rich sheep-farming

[1] Cf. R. Stonor, *Stonor*, p. 259.

counties. Lord Morley of Hallingbury Morley in Essex and Lord Mordaunt of Turvey in Bedfordshire may with their respective heirs, Sir Henry Parker and Sir John Mordaunt, serve as examples.[1] The Mordaunts in particular were very prosperous for they had built the great house of Drayton in this generation. The Morleys and the Mordaunts had no relationship to, and as far as can be discerned, no correspondence with any of the other members of the Catholic gentry.

It would seem that in certain cases, the squires were retained for the old religion by their parish priests. Thus Sir William Dormer, whose daughter was a maid of honour to Queen Mary and later the celebrated Duchess of Feria, had as his vicar at Wing in Buckinghamshire Dr Holyman, a Conservative theologian, who was later the Marian Bishop of Bristol.

A traditional example among the Catholic stocks was that of the Throckmortons of Coughton in Warwickshire. Two heads of the family spanned this period, Sir George who held the estates from 1519 until 1553, and his son Sir George, who succeeded him and survived until 1570. The son in particular was a progressive landlord who made enclosures by agreement with his tenantry. At Coughton could be seen the beginning of an independent Catholic life for the landlords and the holders of surrounding farms.

The influence of such bishops as Gardiner and Tunstall had had much to do with maintaining the attachment to the mass, as had the Conservative character of the older clergy ordained before the breach with Rome. This was also to some extent reflected in the outlook of the clergy of the later Henrican period and among a proportion of the expelled monks, who had accepted parishes.

At the same time, there was little that resembled the influence of the Catholic family priest of later times. Thus two of Sir George's younger sons, who were well-known in the reign of Queen Elizabeth as Sir Clement and Sir Nicholas Throckmorton, adopted a Protestant standpoint which then seemed so suitable for a modern man in touch with the current of thought of the mid-century.

---

[1] Lord Mordaunt had been born before 1485 and Lord Morley in that year. Morley voted in 1549 against the Act for abolishing old prayer books and images.

The Churchwarden's Accounts[1] at Pyrton in Oxfordshire show
how the churches, which had remained untouched through all
King Henry's reign, now suffered alteration. An instruction was
received that all lands or cattle given for the maintenance of lamps
must be surrendered and there was an entry of $4d$ for the cost of
'delyvering of the lampe cow'. This was soon followed by an order
for 'a great white-washing of the Church' to obliterate pictures of
the saints or sacred objects.

As these remarks should make clear Catholicism at this time was
as a force in English secular politics wholly inert. The tendency of
every element was just preservative. The northern farms were
much too far away to have any influence on the London Government. The landowners who were closer to the capital had only the
desire to keep for themselves a private life. Among the members
of the greater peerages there were small groups of men and women
who remained in a certain degree faithful to the old religion;
but this was envisaged principally as an attachment to the mass.
Above all there was, or so it seems to me, no men within the range
of Government who had what could be called a Catholic policy.

A careful study leads one to suppose that there were two families
of the higher peerage who had a strong Catholic attachment
throughout this reign, the Earl of Shrewsbury and Lord Dacres,
and Shrewsbury's daughters and Dacres' children. They made a
close-knit grouping for Shrewsbury, now a widower, had been
married to Mary Dacres and Lord Dacres' wife was Shrewsbury's
sister.

The Earl of Shrewsbury and Lord Dacres were both elderly
men, exact contemporaries, born in the opening year of the sixteenth century. They had both a well-established religious background, Shrewsbury with his private chaplains and Dacres, who
had a close association with the priory of Lanercost. They were
just on thirty before the old *régime* was interrupted. They belonged
to that ancient rooted peerage which Henry VIII had never really
liked: but there was no reason to attack the Earl of Shrewsbury.
He was deeply traditional, a high-minded Regalian. He had supported the King in all his troubles, there was no fault to find with
him. He had been the royal commander against the Pilgrims of

[1] Cf. R. Stonor, *Stonor*, pp. 232–3.

Grace. He had naturally obtained great lands as soon as the monasteries had been suppressed. He had inevitably received the Garter. His great household at Sheffield Castle was almost the centre of a viceroyalty. There was no action that the Crown could take against him for under any circumstances he would always support the King of England.

He was throughout a true conservative; he had a profound conviction, which he shared with the other members of his small high class, of the need for the preservation and accumulation of his hereditary lands. He had observed all the happenings of the last two-thirds of King Henry's reign. His unfortunate sister had been married to the Earl of Northumberland at the time of the Pilgrimage of Grace. He had seen misfortune overtake each member of the White Rose families.

It may be said that in his religious life he had made sacrifices; but these were inevitable for any great man who would serve a Tudor King. He would retain his unimpassioned course. He was no threat to John Dudley or to any other ruler who accepted the position of the upper classes. He looked out very calmly from his northern castle, an old, wise widower. It seems that he had a fellow-feeling for the great possessors and a sober preference for the ancient ways. He died in the first months of the reign of Queen Elizabeth, loyal as ever to his sovereign, and the quiet leader of the Catholic members of the House of Lords.

His daughter Anne was throughout her life, first as Lady Braye and then as Lady Wharton, a fierce Catholic. His son, Lord Talbot, was somewhat separate from his father. He had been born when the Earl was only twenty-one and he had come to a rather different outlook since his marriage with a member of the Manners family, who were deeply Anglican.[1] His Catholic tendencies had faded out and he would, as Earl of Shrewsbury, prove to be a loyal supporter of the policies of Queen Elizabeth.

William, fourth Lord Dacre of Gilsland, known as Lord Dacre of the North,[2] was in a very different position from his wife's brother. He was in a sense outside the Court periphery. A great

---

[1] The sixth earl was born in 1522 and had been married in 1539 to Lady Gertrude Manners. He held the Shrewsbury earldom from 1560 until 1590.
[2] Dacre of the North and Dacre of the South were respectively the heir male and the heir general of the North Country barony.

4 The Duke of Northumberland—no authentic portrait exists but this engraving is based on a portrait found at Penshurst and for a time considered to be of the Duke.

5 Thomas Cranmer,
Archbishop of
Canterbury, a
portrait by Gerhard
Flicke 1552.

6 Bradgate Park, a seventeenth-century engraving of Lady Jane Grey's home.

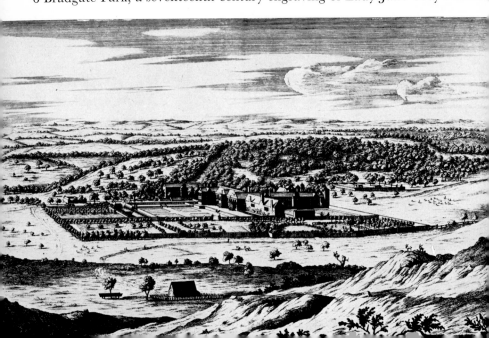

landowner on the Scottish border, he had an hereditary claim to the wardenship of the Western Marches. He also had inherited considerable estates from his mother, in whose right he held the Greystoke barony. He had become warden as a young man in 1527 shortly after his father had died at a great age in falling from his horse. In 1534 he had been tried and acquitted by his peers on a charge of treasonable relations with the Scots. His subsequent employments were of a minor character, but the wardenship of the Western Marches had been restored to him in 1549. He was essentially a 'country peer'. His relationships were with the greater gentry of the North Country, with the Tunstalls of Thurland Castle from whom Bishop Tunstall was derived and with the Parrs of Kendal, the family of Queen Catherine.

His religion seems to have been at a different level from that of Lord Shrewsbury. It was not for him to sit at Sheffield Castle and to detect the seismographic movements of the Court. He had an old-fashioned attachment to the Roman Church rather resembling the type of outlook of Sir Thomas Percy, the young head of that great house, who would in time become the seventh Earl of Northumberland. In 1549 Lord Dacre was among the very few lay peers who voted against permitting the marriage of the clergy and the introduction of the first *Book of Common Prayer*. His children were brought up with a certain strictness, Sir Thomas, who became his successor, and his two daughters. The elder Anne was married in the last months of Henry VIII's reign to the Earl of Cumberland and the younger, Magdalen, later became the wife of Viscount Montagu. In the case of Magdalen there is an isolated piece of information that has some interest. According to her *Life*, written in Latin by Richard Smith, Bishop of Chalcedon, it is stated that at the age of thirteen, presumably upon her mother's death, she was sent 'to the old Countess of Bedford to be brought up a Catholic'.

This raises the question of families divided in religion at this period. Lady Bedford was the widow of Sir Richard Jerningham and had been married to Sir John Russell in 1526 before the coming of the Reformation. It seems that she retained the Catholic faith, while her husband and her children had become decided Protestants.

G

There are two other similar cases. The Duchess of Northumberland, who was Lady Bedford's contemporary, had been married in approximately the same year. Like Anne Jerningham, Jane Guldeford belonged to an old-fashioned grouping of the country squirearchy. In her last years she was certainly a practising Catholic. Is it not likely that she retained these preferences throughout her life? In that generation, before the coming of the Counter-Reformation, a woman would not have been likely to hold out against the views of the head of her family to the extent of conveying her own beliefs to her husband's children.

The final case relates to someone of a rather younger generation. Catherine, Countess of Huntingdon was by birth a Pole and a niece of the Cardinal. She had been brought up as a strict Catholic with a style of piety that was going out of fashion. Her husband had joined the Protestant section of the ruling class and her son would be the famous Puritan Earl of Huntingdon. It seems likely that secretly she retained her Catholic views until they could be brought forward in Queen Mary's reign. We can only grope for information upon this subject. Protestantism was in Edward VI's reign always visible; it is always much more difficult to discover a hidden faith.

III

Emerging Forces

One of the consequences of King Edward's reign was the emergence
of the Protestant Englishman, a type which in his father's time had
been confined for the most part to the lower and middle classes in
the cities and especially in London. This was linked with that up-
surge of Calvinism which was making headway in this reign both
in Scotland and in France. There was a close analogy between the
Huguenot gentry and great nobles in France and their counter-
parts in Edwardian England. Thus the future chief Puritan leader,
the Earl of Huntingdon, was growing up in this reign and so were
those Naval leaders, Sir John Hawkins and Sir Francis Drake.[1] On
the military side, the chief exemplar of this standpoint was to be
Sir Humphrey Gilbert, who was very slightly Drake's senior. He
was lost in a storm to the south of the Azores and was last seen in
the stern sheets of the *Squirrel* with his Bible. It was clear that this
attachment to the Scriptures belonged for the most part to men
who were not accustomed to, and did not care for, reading.
Throughout the Naval history of England there has always been
this Evangelical tradition, in which the dedicated officer restrained
his reading to technical treatises and to careful perusal of the
Bible.

Three different types of man, each with a military background,
had close affinities, the Scottish Presbyterian, the French Huguenot
and their English counterpart. In the spirit of the mid-sixteenth
century, it was natural for a young man to realize that the moulds
of the past were broken. It was inevitable for Calvinism, as opposed
to Lutheranism, to go forward in spite of opposition. This was

---

[1] Lord Huntingdon was born in 1535, Hawkins in 1532 and Drake approximately
in 1540.

particularly the case in those crucial years in France and Scotland. Northumberland belonged to the older generation, to a very different world and outlook. He could not avoid, however, noting the advantages that came with this virile faith.

The sense of the independence of the nation had developed very steadily in English life after the breach with Rome. This separation placed the King's subjects in a new context. The younger generation of the seafarers and the soldiers became politically Protestant, with a varying degree of theological involvement. Among the younger men, it was Spain that was seen as the rival and the enemy. It was this which made the later Marian alliance with Philip II appear bizarre and retrograde.

In politics the future of England was gradually emerging into a situation which would lead to an equal alliance with the French monarchy. It was thus natural that Edward should seek a princess of the House of Valois as his bride. It was a link with France that, like England, she resented the papal division of the new world in the west between the crowns of Spain and Portugal. The young King was wholeheartedly in favour of this alignment. The former alliance with the Emperor, with its memory of the old papal pretensions, was left almost without supporters.

There was therefore much in Northumberland's ideas which was quite popular. He liked most military men and was close in touch with the military mind. He understood the new-found growth of commerce. At the same time, it was his misfortune that he could not hope to rule the English kingdom as what must be termed a rather old-fashioned *condottiere*.

IV

The Continental Scene

Upon the continent this was a calm, autumnal period. The survivor among the great sovereigns, the Emperor Charles V, was drawing towards the close of his long reign. It was a quiet time except for the sharp, brief war along the frontiers of France and Germany. In particular, the lengthy peace in the Netherlands was not yet broken.

Italy was also tranquil. The new French King, Henry II, had given up those Italian ambitions in Milan and in Naples, which had attracted the French sovereigns for half a century. The Italian influence on France was growing weaker. The Emperor's great rival, Francis I, had died in 1547. The Court was no longer dominated by that unquiet monarch with his great nose and his love of architecture and jewels and luxury, the ivory satin of the Clouet portraits.

The Huguenots were now growing in France and that ineradicable alliance was developing that would unite them politically with the German Calvinists. In 1552, as the result of a short war, Lorraine had become detached from Germany and linked to Paris, and the three Bishoprics of Verdun, Toul and Metz had been brought within the orbit of the Valois monarchy. All this was bitter for the old Emperor. He was back now in Flanders, which had been his birth place. The chimerical ambitions for the regaining of the duchy of Burgundy, which was his inheritance, were now ended and it was clear that he was leaving Germany divided in religion. There was no sign as yet of the opening of that Counter-Reformation on which his House would pin its hopes.

A form of Catholicism, rather sluggish and heavy in its emphasis,

lay across the public and private life of the still united Low
Countries. The singing at the Chapel Royal in Brussels, under the
impulse of Charles V's sister and viceroy, the Queen of Hungary,
was now most elaborate. The old Emperor's sympathy was
fastened on the young Prince of Orange, who had been brought
back to Catholicism and regained from his Lutheran parents at
Dillenburg, when he inherited his vast estates. This was the time
of the building of the Palais de Nassau at Brussels for the youthful
prince. The Emperor had guarded this great inheritance which lay
across the country and included the church at Breda among the
sycamores. This was the Catholic period of that great figure who,
as William the Silent, would become the founder of the Calvinistic
Netherlands.

The Queen of Hungary was coming towards the end of her long
viceroyalty begun in 1531. Her headquarters was at Brussels in
the former castle of the Dukes of Brabant. She also spent much
time in her two Italianate hunting lodges at Biche and Mariemont.
This was one of the great ages of the Brussels tapestries. In the new
buildings, the lengthening colonnades and the rows of windows,
with their careful glass-work, were now in place. In the portraits
of this time, the countryside of Brabant is found reflected, while
from this region there had come those riverine landscapes of the
Baptism of Christ by Lucas van Gassel and from an earlier period
that of the *Madonna of the Chancellor Rollin*, now in the Louvre.
The rivers flowed across the picture, rising in the distant hills. It
was all manageable and capable of imitation. This was in keeping
with the festivals of the Southern Netherlands, the *Joyeuse Entrée*
and the *Kermesse Héroicque*. The Low Countries were familiar to the
English merchants as a consequence of the great mart and money
market at Antwerp.

There were considerable resemblances to the French polity, for
in France the actual ruling circle was similarly old-fashioned. The
most important figure was the now ageing Constable de Montmorency. He had a network of connexions across Europe and his
wife, Madeleine de Savoie-Tenda, came from a legitimate branch
of the Savoyard ducal house. He had always had a deep respect
for the Emperor Charles. Both the French and the Imperial
Courts had a detached outlook on the English ruling class, the

managers of a country which had a little run to seed since Henry VIII's time.

There was always a certain difference in religious emphasis. In England Protestantism had come to flower a little early before the same outlook had a chance to ripen in France and the Low Countries, as far as the wealthier classes were concerned. The new Duke of Northumberland was evidently the one key figure.

Ambassadors as yet seldom belonged to a regular service with promotion from post to post, except in the case of those from the Venetian Republic and the nuncios sent out from the Holy See. They were the representatives of dynasties and not of governments; they were essentially members of their own king's ruling circle. Their quality depended on the interests which their posts aroused in their masters' policies. Thus at the time of the death of the Duke of Somerset, the French and Imperialist ambassadors in London were men of little weight, both of them anxious to return to their own countries, René de Laval de Boisdauphin and Jean Scheyfve. It was the despotism of the Duke of Northumberland which aroused the interest of the neighbouring sovereigns and this new concern produced men of a different quality. The contrast was more marked in the case of the Empire, where Scheyfve was replaced by Simon Renard. Both the new ambassadors were by inheritance French-speaking for Renard was from Vesoul in the Franche-Comté, that part of the county of Burgundy which had come down to the Emperor as the representative of the Burgundian dukes. He and his French counter-part Antoine de Noailles were also both politically Catholic.

The policies of the two ambassadors were diametrically opposed. The Emperor was coming towards the end of his long reign and no other Hapsburg ruler would have such an extensive sovereignty. As sovereign of the Netherlands and Spain it was essential that his shipping should have free passage through the Narrow Seas. As France was a foreseen enemy, it was important to have a friendly power to the northward of the Channel. Still, there were difficulties. The strong Protestantism of the English King was uncongenial and it could be imagined that he would do his best to secure a Protestant successor.

In actual fact, the heiress to the throne under the provisions of the will of Henry VIII was his elder sister, the Lady Mary, the first cousin of the Emperor, but it seemed extremely improbable that she would obtain the throne. At the same time it was only for the Spanish Netherlands, whose links of trade were so very close with England, and to a lesser extent for the lands of the Crowns of Spain, that the English alliance, or to what might amount to the absence of English hostility, was of importance.

In addition to his position as Roman Emperor, Charles V had the hereditary lands of his House in Austria and the Tyrol and in South Germany. There were also in more remote control the relatively recent Hapsburg lands, the kingdom of Bohemia and those territories of the kingdom of Hungary which were not yet occupied by the Turks. In Italy the Emperor ruled the duchy of Milan and the kingdom of the Two Sicilies. In the Mediterranean he held Sardinia and the Balearics. Seen thus across the network of his European sovereignties, the hostility or goodwill of the English ruler might seem less significant. At the same time it was not yet evident on what parties in the English State the Lady Mary could call for her support. At the opening of his embassy it can hardly have seemed to Simon Renard that there was very much to hope for from the scene in England.

The situation of the French ambassador was very different. The French Government from the very outbreak of the religious troubles until at least the end of the Cardinal de Richelieu's administration had always kept an open mind in regard to all relations with foreign Protestants. France was the only power whose ruler had seemed to the young Edward VI as an exemplar. The sole foreign order that he received was that of St Michel from the French King. At the same time French policy never found any difficulty in accepting a Protestant succession. The Duke of Northumberland and the young and ailing King would between them arrange the matter. In Germany, as the years went by, the Calvinist princes as a consequence of their opposition to the Emperor would inevitably look for help to the French monarchy. The Protestant candidates to the succession to the English throne were very insular; they had no inherent objection to a political alliance with their southern neighbour. There were already the beginning of relations between the French privateers, largely

Huguenots, and their English counter-parts in opposition to the Spaniards in the western seas.

The French outlook was very practical. They wished to cultivate the goodwill of the Duke of Northumberland as long as that statesman should remain in power. They had no preference among the various puppets whom he might support. It seems likely that Noailles considered that the Protestant forces had already gained control of the English kingdom.

There was, however, one solution which was wholly unacceptable to the representatives of France. At this time it did not seem to be a present danger. This was the accession to the Crown of the Lady Mary, the first cousin to the Emperor. She was devoted to her mother's cause, King Henry's repudiated wife, the Princess of Aragon.

---

[1] It is worth noting that among King Edward's possible successors the young Queen of Scots, grand-daughter and representative of Margaret, Queen of Scotland, King Henry's elder sister, was at this time at the Court of France and soon to be married to the Dauphin. This claim could not have been pressed forward except at the cost of a war with England.

V

The Explorations

It is hard to imagine John Dee as a young man, for we are confused
by the portentous figure that he became in after life, the Dr Dee
with his doctorate in Alchemy, a figure half-famous and half-
notorious, a conjurer of spirits with his great milky beard. It was
the dream of the poor man drawn to science to manufacture gold.
It was a temptation to foretell the future. It was not unreasonable
that Dee should travel to Bohemia. Astrology bore down upon the
Emperor Rudolf and on Dee's patron and partner, the head of the
great house of Rosenberg, who was devoted to extending the
frontiers of knowledge. After all the famous Wenzel Eusebius von
Wallenstein was also fascinated by the hidden secrets of astrology.
Dr Dee was in later life caught up by those temptations to arcane
knowledge. Now he was very different, just a hard-working youth
of twenty-three, rather pushing in his manner and devoted to the
study of the methods of geography.

On his return from France at the end of 1550 Dee entered into
the Duke of Northumberland's service. At first he was employed
in teaching Lord John Dudley the application of mathematics to
the art of warfare. Rather later he dedicated a book on astronomy
to the Duchess of Northumberland, one of the rare references to
this self-effacing lady.

In some ways the ideas fostered by Northumberland suggest a
foretaste of the Elizabethan Age. This was because in terms of sea
adventure Spain was already seen as the victim and the enemy;
France, on the contrary, appeared to Northumberland in terms of
friendship. It is worth noting that French interests in colonial
development, like the colony projected and finally set up in Florida,
would be very largely in the hands of Huguenots. The whole sea

movement was in those days towards the Tropics. The northern journeys were intended in the end to lead men southwards. There was a conviction that gold lay only in the hot countries and that there were no minerals in the frozen North.

Apart from the North-West and North-East Passages every voyage in search of new trade would come up against the vast regions already claimed by Spain or Portugal. There were certain differences between these nations. There was as yet no sign of the end of the Portuguese dynasty of the House of Aviz and there were always a few Portuguese pilots who were ready to guide English ships in these far waters. Impressions of foreign parts were very vague. Thus Richard Eden (born 1521) was to give an account of the land of Africke, of Mauritania Tingitana and Mauritania Caesariensis, of the kingdoms of Marocca and Fez and their divisions. He did not fail to mention David the Emperor of Ethiopia and his province of Manicongo, 'whose king is a Moore, and tributary to the Emperour.[1] In this province are manie exceeding high mountaines, upon the which is said to be the earthly Paradise.'[2]

The first voyages to the Gold Coast and the Grain Coast had been planned under the rule of the Duke of Northumberland. They had been immediately preceded by the first beginnings of the Morocco trade. This was an inevitable development of the voyages both to the Canaries and the Azores which had taken place throughout the later years of King Henry's reign. The initiation of the regular Barbary trade appears to date from 1551.

The first voyage was commanded by Thomas Wyndham, who was master of the ordnance of the King's ships, and had acted as Vice-Admiral under Lord Clinton in charge of the royal vessels sent to the coast of Scotland. He had served with the Duke when he was Lord Admiral and was a first cousin to the Duke of Somerset but, like most of his class, he had rallied easily to Northumberland. He was captain and part-owner of the *Lion* of London, which made 'the first voyage of traficque into the kingdom of Marocco in Barbarie'. This enterprise had been financed by Sir John

[1] David II, otherwise Lebna Dengel, who ruled from 1508 until 1540.
[2] Printed by Richard Hakluyt in *Principal Navigations, Voyages and Discoveries*, ed. D. B. Quinn (1965), vol. i, pp. 84–5.

Luttrell of Dunster, who was Wyndham's neighbour and relative,[1] and by Henry Ostrich, a London merchant. Both these supporters died of the Great Sweat shortly before the ships got under way. The details of this voyage do not appear to have been preserved.[2] In the next year he sailed again to Barbary in the *Lion* with two other ships in company. This voyage was promoted by Sir John Yorke,[3] Sir William Garrard, Sir Thomas Wroth and Francis Lambert, a *consortium* based on London. The ships called at Zafia (now Saffi) and at Santa Cruz (now Agadir). They obtained a cargo of sugar, molasses, dates and almonds. A regular trade was then set up. The English vessels bringing English cloth and quantities of arms and munitions and taking back a large amount of gum, which was used for the processes of cloth-finishing.

Immediately linked with this trade was the first voyage to the coast of Guinea. This was wild land described as where the deserts reach the Ocean Sea. This expedition was set out in the spring of 1553 and was under the command of Thomas Wyndham. Fortunately, there exists a portrait which represents him, a large full-bodied figure with a black beard.[4] He died too young for much to be learned about him.

He again sailed in the *Lion* and took with him the *Primrose* and the *Moon*, a pinnace, both hired from the Royal Navy. These ships made the passage southwards and reached the Gold Coast, their crews landing a little to the eastward of the fortress of Elmina. From the neighbouring chiefs they gained one hundred and fifty pounds of gold. They then pressed onwards to the Gulf of Benin, where Wyndham and many of his crew died of fever. The *Lion* and the *Moon* were abandoned on this coast and the *Primrose* came back to England with the survivors.

Still the discovery of gold and the English intervention, which was soon to develop, in the trade in slaves between Africa and the West Indies and South America never seems to have been of much concern to the Duke of Northumberland. Unlike Elizabeth I, he

[1] For the connexions of Thomas Wyndham, cf. *A Family History, 1410–1688, the Wyndhams of Norfolk and Somerset* by H. A. Wyndham (1939), pp. 53–8.
[2] Cf. an interesting account in *Sir John Hawkins, the Time and the Man*, by James A. Williamson (1927), pp. 34–41.
[3] Sir John Yorke was the patron of Martin Frobisher, who made his first voyage to Guinea.
[4] Painted in 1550 by Hans Ewouts and now in the possession of the Earl of Radnor.

never invested in such foreign traffic. It was a very different matter from the problem af the Passage to Cathay. This was in essence a question of geography and mathematics, which opened out upon a broad strategical conception.

The question of the North-East and North-West Passages had this advantage. Here we are dealing not with imagination, but with a distorted appreciation of reality. Both would in fact have been practicable at certain seasons, if ice-breakers had been developed at this time. Given the knowledge of those days, it seems strange that seamen did not fear that western Canada, in fact Alaska, might be joined by a land-bridge to Siberia. The ice-laden waters of the Bering Straits, which separate the continents, were not to be discovered until Vitus Bering came there in 1728. There is no doubt that in considering the two alternatives the North-West Passage would seem preferable.

The protagonist of this voyage was Sebastian Cabot, a man of seventy-six, who had passed over twenty years as pilot-major to the King of Spain. He was of mixed descent and born at Bristol, to which port he returned, when he entered the King of England's service in the first months of Edward's reign.[1] There is no surviving account of Sebastian Cabot's voyage, which had taken place as long ago as 1509. Dr J. A. Williamson has done much scholarly work in disentangling the history of this family. What matters here is the account of the farthest point of his travels, which the younger Cabot gave.

Sebastian Cabot made it clear that he did not land upon Newfoundland, which his father had discovered, but made his way bearing to the westward of the coast of Labrador, as Greenland was then termed. He reached through what is now the Hudson Strait to the opening of that great sheet of water, which afterwards was known as Hudson Bay. There was a certain amount of ice, but he had penetrated to what appeared to him to be the open ocean. Away to the south there stretched the wide smooth seas under a leaden sky. In the far distance there was a sea horizon. It was summer in the high latitudes. Beyond these waters there

[1] Sebastian's father seems to have been a Genoese and his mother was of Venetian stock. Cf. J. A. Williamson, *The Voyages of the Cabots* (1929) and an excellent analysis of the problem, *The Voyage of John and Sebastian Cabot* printed in 1937 for the Historical Association.

must lie those southward-bearing straits which marked the Passage to Cathay. As the ships moved onwards, the weather would become first temperate and then warm as they sailed on across the ocean to the hot Chinese lands. This was the picture that he always painted; behind him stood the Bristol Venturers.

The next project, the discovery of a North-East Passage, owed its conception to John Dee. He had come back to England with the astronomer's ring of brass and the astronomer's staff likewise of brass given him by the geographer, Gemma Frisius, and also with two great globes constructed by Gerard Mercator. He was also in contact with a practical navigator, Richard Chancellor, who had been educated in Sir Henry Sidney's household. The voyage, which was now in prospect, had two parts. While the making of the North-West Passage was a journey which should result in commerce, that of the North-East Passage began with a diversion to Moscow, to open the Russian lands to the export trade in heavy woollens. It was only when this had been achieved that the actual passage would be begun.

These were the geographical implications. Dee, and those who followed his advice, were ignorant both of the great length of the northern coast of Siberia and also of the condition of the Arctic Seas. They had naturally not heard of the big land mass of Novaya Zemlya which lay across the eastern frontiers of the Barendts Sea. This forbidding land stretched northwards for six hundred miles of fiords, islands and bays from the North Russian coast into the Arctic regions. It was divided half-way up its length by the winding channel the Matochkin Shar and at its southern end it was separated from the mainland by the Ugrian Strait; but both these waters would be blocked by ice.

Novaya Zemlya was a high, wind-swept land, uninhabited and crowned by snow fields, from which great glaciers slipped down to the sea. The expedition was to reach it in late August when Goose Land, which they sighted, was covered by coarse grasses and the masses of sharp-coloured flowers were still in bloom. The Russians never considered this as a through-way and detailed exploration of Novaya Zemlya did not take place until the reign of Catherine II, in the late eighteenth century.

This expedition was the last that would sail from England,

while the Duke of Northumberland was still its ruler. It was the last attempt that would be made to find the North-East Passage. Ice-laden fogs wreathed down on the quiet northern sea. At intervals along the coast of Novaya Zemlya lay icebergs, which the eastward-bearing current had stranded there.

The admiral in command of the three ships was Sir Hugh Willoughby, a cadet of the great family of Willoughby of Wollaton. His flagship was the *Bona Esperanza*. The general pilot of the expedition was Richard Chancellor in the *Bonaventure Edward*. The flagship, with the *Confidentia* in company, reached the northern port of Vardohuus, where they had agreed to meet; but they never found the *Bonaventure Edward*. It seems that they turned towards the west; the two ships, with Willoughby and both their companies dead in them, were found much later in a Lapland harbour. They had sailed from the London River in May 1553 and sighted Novaya Zemlya three months later. After that the northern winter came down upon them.[1]

The general planning of the voyage had been Dee's work. The Company of the Merchant Venturers of England had sent them forth and Sebastian Cabot was their technical adviser. He had favoured the North-Eastern journey on account of the importance of the trade with Moscow, the heavy woollens. The *Bonaventure Edward* entered the White Sea and anchored at the Russian village of Archangelsk. Carrying letters from King Edward, Chancellor set off for the Court of Muscovy. It seems that he was the first Englishman to visit there. Still, contacts had been maintained with Western Europe for the Hanseatic League had long kept up a carefully-guarded trade route, which ran from Riga by way of Novgorod to Moscow. There had also been elaborate embassies from the nearest Western Power, the Crown of Poland. Ivan IV the Terrible was then in the earlier portion of his long reign.[2]

Chancellor and his companions rode southwards on the post horses which the Tsar had sent to meet them, through the open champaign country and the forests filled with fir trees. The account of Moscow has interest. The patriotic flavour should be discounted,

---

[1] They had left England so as to gain the summer weather. It is not explained why they did not return during the autumn.
[2] Ivan IV succeeded in 1533 and died in 1584.

but it shows how Moscow struck those who were familiar with Tudor London. 'And because,' wrote Clement Adam in his narrative,[1] 'the citie of Mosco is the chiefest of all the rest, it seemeth of itself to challenge the first place in this discourse. Our men say that in bignes it is as great as the Citie of London, with the Suburbes thereof. There are many and great buildings in it, but for beauty and fairnes, nothing comparable to ours. . . . Their streetes and waies are not paved with stone as ours are: the walles of their houses are of wood; the roofes for the most part are covered with shingle boordes.' The Castle has a great brick wall ; 'in the Castle there are nine Churches or Chapels, not altogether unhansome. As for the King's Court and Pallace, it is not of the neatest, onely in forme it is four square, and of lowe building. The windowes are very narrowly built and some of them by glasse, some others by lattices admitte the light.' Adam points out that there were neither tapestries nor hangings in the palace. He describes the dresses of the courtiers, the cloth of gold, the sables and the furs. By implication, for he makes no open statement, there was no market for heavy woollens here. The rich would never need them and the poor were not in a position to make a purchase.

It would appear that it was the geographical aspect of these journeys which principally aroused Northumberland's practical concern; but it should be noted that in the early 1550s the boom in English cloth exports came to an end and there was in consequence a major crisis in the cloth trade, affecting in particular London and the Merchant Adventurers trading to Antwerp. It is worth noting that this factor had its importance on the voyages of both commerce and exploration which have just been described.

It may be contended that Northumberland also attempted to bring about a partial restoration of the coinage. The 'Great Debasement'[1] of the currency, which had begun under Henry VIII, does not fall within the scope of the present study.

[1] The Voyages and the Discoveries of Richard Chancellor printed in *The Principall Navigations, Voyages and Discoveries of the English Nation* by Richard Hakluyt, ed D. B. Quinn and R. A. Skelton (1965), pp. 286–7.
[1] Cf. J. D. Gould, *The Great Debasement*, 1970.

VI

The Palatinate of Durham

It seems that it was the situation of Cuthbert Tunstall, Bishop of Durham, which first set the Duke of Northumberland's mind on the rich Palatinate in the north. There was never any question of building up a great proprietorship on lands which had belonged to his fellow-peers. It was the Church lands which alone could be used with convenience to build up the complex of his ducal territories.

It was the moderation of Bishop Tunstall's opposition which had preserved his position until this time. Unlike Bishop Gardiner, he had had no part in the swing of politics at King Henry's Court. He was now very old. In any case, he was not the sort of man whom Dudley liked; but he was very difficult to dislodge. He was a true Regalian. In one way, for a later age, it is less difficult than in other instances to appreciate and understand him. He had a natural horror of suffering and in particular of an ignominious and painful death. But where he differed from men of his own time was in his dislike of causing pain to others. It does not seem that, throughout his long life, he was ever primarily responsible for the burning of a single heretic.

He had a general and a diffused good will. He was himself a high conservative, but it was perhaps the fact that he had broken with the Papacy which led him to sympathize with those whose theological speculations were much more radical than his own. He was an aged man who had sympathy with the younger generation and, in especial, with the Duke of Somerset. Cranmer was fifteen years his junior and his old and faithful friend.

Years had eroded the conservative prelates of the reign's beginning. Seven bishops had joined Tunstall in voting against the

H

first Prayer Book in 1549. Thirlby, who was also of his opinion, was at that time absent. Bishop Rugg of Norwich was now dead. Bonner, Heath and Day had in the interval suffered deprivation. Among the other prelates of that way of thinking only Thirlby, who had succeeded Rugg at Norwich, and Aldrich of Carlisle still kept their sees. With them may be counted two other Conservative bishops of less account, Anthony Kitchin, the very old and weak Bishop of Landaff, and Paul Bush, Bishop of Bristol, who was himself a married man.

While Archbishop Cranmer's position was weakening in the State, among the churchmen it was growing stronger. With only a couple of exceptions, the old Henrican bishops had now passed away from active life except for Latimer, who in those days had been a rebel. The Archbishop's mind was now bent on the question of Reformation unity; he envisaged a union of the Reformed Confessions. His leadership in the Protestant world of Europe was growing stronger. In 1552 he had suffered from ill health and had two illnesses. He was engaged in producing his second Prayer Book, where the influences that now beat on him were clearly seen. For instance, in the administration of the Sacrament, the term 'priest' was now replaced by that of 'minister'. But there was no time for these measures to have their effect. They would all be swept away when Northumberland's *régime* was destroyed.

Meanwhile, these activities had no effect on the great Duke. Northumberland was not interested in divines' opinions. He wanted only one thing from Bishop Tunstall, that was his land.[1]

It is not easy to reconstruct just what Tunstall looked like. His long residence in the north resulted in his not coming within the range of Holbein's brush. There appear in fact to be only two portraits which may be held to represent him. The picture at Burton Constable in Yorkshire, done (if it really is his portrait) when he was young, has little interest. The portrait at Greatworth Manor has a certain power. This is a head and shoulders, full face, painted in his later years. He is wearing a dark gown and a large black head-gear. His grey hair turning white is shown curl-

[1] It should be mentioned that the Duke of Somerset had shown the way in his dealings with the see of Bath and Wells, cf. P. Hembry, *The Bishops of Bath and Wells, 1540–1600* (1967).

ing on his forehead. Rather far down his substantial nose there rests a pair of black spectacles, modern in their appearance. He is reading a large book with iron clasps.[1]

There is a certain hesitation about his origins. He appears to have been the son of Thomas Tunstall of Thurland Castle in Lancashire, the head of his stock. His mother, to whom Thomas Tunstall was not married, seems to have been a Conyers of Hackforth in the North Riding. From an early age he was fully accepted by the family and when he was a young ecclesiastic he was made guardian to Marmaduke Tunstall, who inherited Thurland Castle in 1513 when he was a child.[2]

As this detail indicates Bishop Tunstall's position was in some respects unique. He alone among King Henry's later bishops had belonged since childhood to that world of the greater squirearchy, which had such influence at the royal court. This may perhaps explain how any man of the same background, like the Earl of Southampton of the first creation and his half-brother Sir Anthony Browne, would attempt to bring him in to some high place, perhaps the Chancellorship, at the fall of Cardinal Wolsey and again when Thomas Cromwell's power began to crumble.

The Bishop had been a friend to Sir Thomas More and he does not seem to have wished to come too close to the royal person. He held a great post connected with the see of Durham as the first Lord President of the Council of the North, and before and after he had gone on embassies. As long as King Henry lived he seems to have been happy to represent the English Church and the English Crown at foreign courts. He had studied at Padua in his youth and he had a close knowledge of European history. He was very learned. Throughout Henry VIII's time it was apparent that the essential Catholic doctrines and the sacrifice of the Mass remained intact. Many bishops in the past had served a sovereign who, from time to time, was excommunicate.

All this was now behind him; his friends were dead. In the autumn of 1542 he had anointed Lord Southampton as he lay dying at Newcastle-on-Tyne. He had outlived his contemporaries

[1] Reproduced in C. Sturge, *Life of Cuthbert Tunstall*. It is attributed by this author to Hans Aspen and was at Greatworth Manor in 1938.
[2] The Bishop's ancestry is discussed in Sturge, *op. cit.*, cf. Whitaker's *Richmondshire*, ii, pp. 271–4.

and had no affinity. It could not have seemed to Northumberland that Tunstall would prove a difficult man to strip of his possessions.

These possessions were glittering enough. The great Palatinate of Durham was annexed to the bishopric. It was the last of the palatinates not united to the Crown, for those attached to the earldom of Chester and the duchy of Lancaster had long formed part of the sovereign's appanage. The Palatinate of Durham extended to the whole of that county and also included Norhamshire, Islandshire and Bedlingtonshire in Northumberland, and Allertonshire and Howdenshire in the North Riding. The rights of the jurisdiction included all base metals and coals. The men of the Bishopric had no part in the King's Parliament and coin had been minted at Durham as late as 1536. These rights were in some cases archaic and they certainly would soon be swept away. As it was, the King already exercised the bishop's rights during each vacancy of the see. Unless he gained the lands of the Palatinate, the Duke of Northumberland would be without those great estates which such a dukedom made appropriate.

In May 1551, the case was opened with a charge against Bishop Tunstall of misprision of treason, arising from his recent contacts with the Duke of Somerset. The Bishop was instructed to come south and was ordered to stay at Coldharbour in Thames Street, his London house. The former mansion in the capital, Durham House, had been pared from the diocese in previous years. It was made sufficiently clear to the aged prelate that what the Duke required from him was his bishopric and not his life.

In December of the same year he was removed to the Tower, where he was joined by his chief collaborator James Whitehead, who had been the last prior of the monastery at Durham, and had, since the Suppression, been the Dean. The proceedings were curiously dilatory. On 28 March 1552, a bill for Tunstall's deprivation was introduced in the House of Lords. In this chamber there were only two votes against the Government's proposals. The greater peers, even the Traditionalists, had never had much contact with the old Bishop of Durham; they were not likely in such a matter to oppose the Duke's desires. The one layman who voted against the prosecution was Lord Stourton, a young and obscure peer, who curiously enough was the Duke's nephew. Not much is known of him. He was of a choleric disposition and was hanged in the next reign for murdering his steward. The other objector was of much more importance, the Archbishop of Canterbury. He had always liked Dr Tunstall and was inclined to act with independence, as far as Northumberland was concerned.

Three days later the bill was sent down to the House of Commons and there the members asked for the attendance of the Bishop 'and his accessories'. This was refused and in the following autumn he was tried by a court presided over by the Chief Justice of the King's Bench, sitting at Whitefriars on Tower Hill. In consequence he was deprived of his see. The bishopric of Durham was dissolved by Act of Parliament in March 1553. By this time other troubles had assailed Northumberland.

VII

The Religious Background

Leaving aside the field which was explicitly theological, it is evident that the old worldly position of the bishops inherited from the Mediaeval Church must be destroyed, if this was to synchronize with the Duke of Northumberland's seizure of the lands of the Palatinate of Durham. At the same time, it is necessary to remember that the Duke had by no means a free hand for he must make his own actions accord with the religious views of his young sovereign. These had been fixed for several years before the Duke had come to his full power.

An aura then surrounded the outlook of those two pious sovereigns, Henry VIII and his only son. This was a consequence of the way in which the Tudor monarchy had come to be presented. Men had been brought up to believe that the King would think for them on those high themes. With Edward, and in close touch with him, was the Archbishop of Canterbury. The Duke and the Primate had never had much in common. Still, Northumberland must have known that in any matter of public policy he could bend the Primate to accept his will.

Besides, the Duke had never shown much interest in the various foreign theologians, who had been brought to England by Dr Cranmer and lodged at Lambeth. As far as he was concerned with any foreigners, it was the geographers, whose purely mundane researches roused his concern, these and the mercenary captains of his Italian soldiers, who had been in the royal service during the reign.

The flood of foreigners, whether hopeful theologians or merely exiles, had begun under the Duke of Somerset and had been a main preoccupation of Archbishop Cranmer. As far as Northum-

berland's foreign policy was concerned, they were irrelevant. He
was pledged to a policy of peace with France and they, for the
most part, came from the Spanish Netherlands and from the
western borderlands of the Empire. Apart from the very few who
were admitted to the universities, they settled for the most part in
London. They were often skilled craftsmen, who were clearly
useful there.

As an example, their leader John a Lasco, the celebrated Polish
Reformer, had been superintendent for some years of the churches
dependent on Emden and had come to England in 1549, when the
reigning Countess of East Friesland had moved back towards the
Roman obedience. There was quite a close contact with Emden
and he had already been in touch with English Reformers for
several years. He was given the church of the dissolved monastery
of Austin Friars as a German church, and the large chapel of
St Anthony in Threadneedle Street was assigned to the immigrant
Walloon community. There was, moreover, the King's deep
interest in the care of all the churches. Edward always took such
matters seriously and received the praise accorded to him as an
Angelic Prince with satisfaction. Brought up as an Henrican
courtier, it never seems to have occurred to Northumberland, in
such matters, to do anything except support his sovereign's wishes.

The first episcopal appointment which can be directly traced to
Northumberland was that of John Hooper to the see of Gloucester.
He had recently returned from Zurich and had been acting as
chaplain to the Duke of Somerset. Among all the new prelates he
was the most opposed to the idea of the old mediaeval bishoprics.
In the same year Nicholas Ridley received the diocese of London.
There is little doubt that these two bishops did more than any
others to introduce the novel doctrines; Ridley worked on the
already strong Protestant element in Essex and in the capital,
and Hooper planted the new religion in the relatively untouched
areas along the Severn. Like the general body of his courtier class
Northumberland had little wish to hear their sermons. He had in
fact but little contact with them. As proof of this, Hooper at the
King's death came out in favour of the Lady Mary. On this level
Northumberland had only one desire to procure for himself the
rich endowments of the see of Durham.

Northumberland had close contacts with one divine, who if not strictly a foreigner came from outside the boundaries of the kingdom, Mr Knox, who in time would be the great Scottish Reformer. He was resident in England throughout this reign and was for a time the Duke's chaplain and proposed by him for the bishopric of Rochester, a preferment which he did not accept.[1] In this case it may be that his forthright language and intensely masculine character appealed to Northumberland. In any case it was a liking that was not returned.

It was at the beginning of the period of the Duke's control that the new Prayer Book and the second Act of Uniformity passed through Parliament without difficulty. This was in January 1552 when the reign had only a year and some months to run.

There was at this time a certain privacy in the forms of devotion which now developed. In particular this applied to the wealthy element among the stricter Protestants. There does not seem much reflection in public life of the prayer meetings and preachings that took place in the household and in the family circle of a nobleman of the new strict opinions. This Puritan quality would be found in some of the high Edwardian families. An example is to be found in the life of Lady Jane Grey as a girl.

There was here an English Calvinism, which was never destined to be 'established', unlike the position that developed in the kingdom of Scotland. Viewed from one angle, the situation in the ruling world in Southern England was quite remarkably fissiparous. There were the pockets of rigid Protestantism and the pockets of Catholicism, and then all the various shades of the disintegrating standpoint of Henry VIII's days.

Beside the holders of these various traditions, all in some degree antagonistic to one another, there were also those to whom the conflicting denominations meant little.

Thus it seems that Thomas Cromwell, for all the alloy of personal ambition, was solely dominated by the notion of the service of the State. Religion paled before this deep intention. Two statesmen in France and Scotland had some resemblance to this standpoint in their motive power, Michel de l'Hôpital and Mait-

[1] He received quite towards the end of the reign, on 2 February 1553, the London vicarage of All Hallows, Bread Street.

land of Leathington. A clear indifference in religious matters was a standpoint that no wise man would admit to in that battling century. Those who were suspected or half-suspected of indifference were often to be termed the Machiavellians.

When one has left behind the small band of the sceptics, one comes upon a larger body, men who seem to have had in their hearts either a comatose or sometimes a positive neutrality. One should never fail to allow for the mass of those who were indifferent. In France, in particular, there was a great penumbra of indifference when the Huguenots and the Catholics were first organized against each other. This was reflected later in the *politiques* and was finally embodied in the spirit of the Seigneur de Montaigne.

This situation existed despite the fact that one religious label or another was employed, a consequence of that believing period. In England this position was reflected, but much more faintly. Both at King Henry's Court and at King Edward's, there were men who had at heart a complete indifference to all these questions. This at any rate is how the situation appears to me.

In all ages there have been those whose acceptance of received beliefs was merely formal; but at this period I mean in certain cases something more definite than that. After all, if one examines the matter with detachment, it must seem likely that there were men whose attachment to the old religion had broken down and who yet remained unconvinced by the differing nostrums which the Reformation leaders now set before them. One never can be positive about such matters, but it seems that this may well have been the standpoint of Sir William Petre. It is clear that he was ready to give his services for whatever object the State might seek them. This was, perhaps, in great part due to the high prestige of the Tudor monarchy. The English virtue of patriotism had its play here.

In this particular instance, Petre was a new, great landowner. He had acquired from the monastic properties a very large estate in Henry VIII's time. But it is his frame of mind which will be considered. He was a man of mature years, he had his skills. He was now Secretary of State and his talents were at the service of Northumberland's new Government.

VIII

The Secretary of State

The character of Sir William Petre, of Torbryan in the county of Devon, is difficult to trace and in some respects still indecipherable. In considering his case, it is necessary to forget the later history of the Petre family. Their attachment to the Church of Rome, which would remain inviolable, did not begin until the marriage of Sir William Petre's son with Mary Waldegrave, who was a recusant, in the middle of the reign of Queen Elizabeth. Henceforward, they were to be the stormy petrels of the Roman Church. The great hulk of Thorndon Hall is the monument of this later family.

King Henry's reign had proved fair weather for Sir William Petre. By inheritance he was of well-established yeoman stock. His father, a wealthy farmer, is also said to have been a tanner. He came from Torbryan, in that soft country where the view stretches away to the southward, towards Marldon and the sea. At some distance in the background lies the long line of the moors.

William Petre was born about 1505 and as a young man became a Fellow of All Souls. He had been tutor to Anne Boleyn's brother and early gained the favour of both Cromwell and Cranmer. The beginning was thus almost accidental. He was not a friend to these men or to their separated policies, he was an instrument. He was among the most energetic of the visitors of the lesser monasteries and later also of the greater houses.

The portrait by an unknown hand painted when he was forty, and now at Ingatestone, gives a clear impression. He is wearing a flat black cap with tassels. His dress is all of black with white linen showing at the neck and wrists. On his fourth finger is the Secretary's signet set with a Tudor rose. His eyes are steadfast and

instinct with caution. There is the faintest pencilling of a mous-
tache. He was a close-visaged man; he kept his counsel.

Sir William Petre made a great career of the second rank aided
by a swift appreciation of all worldly changes. His duty was to
serve the Crown of England. He had an unimportant member-
ship of the House of Commons; he never seems to have wished to
be a member of the House of Lords. He had none of that harshness
which attached itself to some of the visitors of the monasteries. He
was always calm with those who never had a chance to move
against him. His origin and his main work had been in Devonshire, but in later life he went to live in Essex. The house at Ingatestone, in which he settled, was one of the outlying properties of
the dissolved abbey of St Mary's, Barking.

Sir William's great riches came to him before the development
of his career in politics. His marriages had both been prudent. His
first with the child of Sir John Tyrrell of Warley had not lasted
long. She left him with two daughters and he then married Anne
Tyrrell, the widow of his first wife's cousin. She was the daughter
of Sir William Browne, Lord Mayor of London, and brought him
a commercial fortune. Henceforth his life was passed between
London and Essex. His associates were in general the country
gentlemen of medium fortune.

As early as 1544 he had rented a small house in Aldersgate
Street, quite close to the water-steps beside Paul's Wharf.[1] In the
same year he bought three adjoining houses and then another
four, which had been part of the property of St Bartholomew's
Priory. It seems that he had intended to build upon this spot, but
in the next year he first rented and then bought a much larger
building from the Drapers' Company, which lay between Long
Lane and Little Britain. Together with the two adjacent tenements,
which had belonged to the *Swan*, this formed the site of Sir William
Petre's new town house. The garden extended to the brick wall
of Lord Rich's mansion, which had been the residence of the
Prior of St Bartholomew's.

The house contained extensive accommodation. The actual list
of rooms comes from an inventory made in 1562, but they seem to

[1] For details about these various buildings, cf. E. G. Emmison, *Tudor Secretary* (1970),
pp. 82–5.

have been the same as in Sir William's first construction.[1] There was a hall and dining chamber, outer and inner great chambers, great and little parlours and a chapel. The interior gallery on the first floor, which led to the private study, was floored with plaster of Paris. Sir William's own bedchamber had a walnut bed with a tester of cloth tissue. This had chequered silver hangings fringed with red and white silk. The walls were tapestried with a rich Arras worked with a pastoral design of crimson flowers.

It was indeed a rich man's house, one of the biggest constructed at that time within the City. It belonged essentially to the character of King Henry VIII's reign, far removed from those great houses which the aristocracy would build along the Strand in the Elizabethan period. Sir William seems to have used it for frequent visits; he does not appear to have ever lived there. It was useful for his duties at the Court, a short passage from the water-steps to Westminster and a longer journey down the stream to Greenwich Palace. It seems that Lady Petre was attached to her City home, but then she had spent her childhood in a London house.

There is a small point which may be mentioned here. In November 1548 Sir William paid 5s. towards the cost of a copy of the new translation of Erasmus' *Paraphrases of the New Testament* for St Botolph-without-Aldersgate, his parish church. He followed with exactitude each instruction in religious matters which successive Governments might give to him. It can be said with perfect truth that his religion was dictated to him by the Crown of England.

There was always a great calm in his approaches. He did not leave Somerset for Northumberland until the former's fall was certain and he remained among the supporters of Lady Jane as long as did all those who would abandon her. He worked out as Secretary the actual details of the settlement of the Crown on Lady Jane and in a similar fashion he produced the details of the Spanish marriage treaty in Queen Mary's reign. He supported the various forms of Protestantism under Edward VI; he obtained a bull from the Pope securing him his former monastic lands in Queen Mary's time; he remained a quiet Anglican under Elizabeth.

It does not seem necessary to accuse him of insincerity. As a boy

---

[1] Emmison, *op. cit.*, p. 83.

he was presumably a Catholic, one cannot tell. In his maturity he was very probably one of those who did not find it necessary to believe in the conflicting versions of the Christian faith which were brought forward.

There are two comments which should be made on the political situation at that time in England. In the sixteenth century no politician would have felt himself bound to support an administration which had not secured its hold upon the country. This would apply to the rule of Protector Somerset in its later stages and still more to the Government of Lady Jane. As a corollary no serious political figure would fail to support a legal Government in the English State.

There is in this especial case another factor. These changes must for any man have been a strain. It seems to me that he turned his mind away from the whole subject. No wonder that in his later years he settled down to study the fruiting of his cherry trees.

Ingatestone Hall, which he spent his last years in building and improving was in its general conception an old-fashioned manor house. It lay upon a gentle slope, surrounded on three sides by orchards. There were many rooms and a great mass of chimneys. From 1549, when the new constructions began, all the windows were glazed except for the mill house, which had wooden latticed windows as in mediaeval days. In the south-west corner of the orchard there was a summer house or small pavilion in which the sweet or fruit course of a dinner might be served in summer. Here life went forward very tranquilly; it was a refuge from all politics.

I

The Succession

Northumberland's conspiracy turned on the matter of the succession to the throne. By a strange chance all those who could be considered to have some claim upon this great inheritance were women. The only man within this circle, Henry VIII's nephew, the young King of Scotland, had died some years before. To give their names in the order of their claim in common law these were the Ladies Mary and Elizabeth, Edward VI's sisters, and then the young Queen of Scotland, who was married to the Dauphin, and her aunt Lady Margaret Douglas, Countess of Lennox.

These last two represented King Henry's elder sister Margaret, but they had been excluded from the succession by his will on the ground that they were foreigners. There came next the representatives of his younger sister, the Queen of France. These were her elder daughter the Marchioness of Dorset and her three girls, and Lady Margaret Clifford, who was the only child of her younger daughter the Countess of Cumberland, who had died in 1547.

It is simplest to examine the possibilities in the order of their claim. The first was the Lady Mary. When the King should die, the Duke might swing his influence in favour of her. There is no reason to suppose that he would have been disturbed by the religious implications of this succession; but his whole great properties were in the process of being built up on the wreck of the estates of the see of Durham. His very title, Northumberland, was likely to prove offensive to her conservative old-fashioned mind. There was, for instance, always the Percy family. It was not easy to see how these difficulties could be resolved to his advantage. There would be nothing to rely on except that by his act he had secured the throne for her. This course of action would in fact have been both over-prudent and very timid. When could North-umberland have been accused of prudence or timidity?

The next in order was the Lady Elizabeth. She was only twenty, a courageous girl. It would be simple to present her as the heiress to the throne, calling in aid King Henry's divorce from the Princess of Aragon. It seems probable, bearing in mind their later relations, that she would have been fascinated by Northumberland's son, Lord Robert Dudley. His marriage with Amy Robsart was not successful and it seems likely that it could have been dissolved. Lord Robert would then have married the new Queen. Of course the continuance of the Duke's power would have been to some extent dependent on the fidelity of his son. There were also two further problems. Could King Edward have been brought to nominate her and would the Lady Elizabeth have agreed? Rejecting both alternatives, the Duke decided in favour of promoting Lady Dorset's daughter, Lady Jane Grey. The succession by the Scottish line was unacceptable, the Dauphine of France could be ruled out and so could Lady Lennox. The new Queen of England must be both young and nubile.

Northumberland possessed that *condottiere* outlook which regarded women as ciphers in the field of politics. It is of interest to speculate as to his sex life. Not only is there no reference to any mistress, but when he came to power no bastard son emerged. The Duke had a prolific, faithful wife. Women seem to have lain outside the range of his political enquiry. Lady Jane Grey had one great advantage. The young King, in order to preserve the Protestant religion, was prepared to bequeath the Crown by will to her. The ties which bound the young people together were outside the range of the Duke's interests.

And in this matter of Lady Jane Grey, it seems worth discussing the effect of the religious changes on the educated section of the world of women. There was a sharp distinction between the Lutheran approach and that of the newer form of the reformed religion, associated with Zwingli and with Calvin, which can in general be grouped as Calvinism. The first was German in its origin, positive and rather heavy. It had come about in gradual stages; it had little fire.

The Court of Brandenburg may serve as an example. The

Elector, Joachim II, had had a somewhat Henrican period before finally accepting Lutheranism. His two wives, the daughters respectively of Duke George of Saxony and the King of Poland, had both retained the Catholic Faith. The permission for a chapel for the second wife may have been in great part due to her high rank. The Dowager Electress survived until 1575. A haze, a profitable haze, hung over the religion of the electoral children through all this time. There were neighbouring bishoprics to which the House of Hohenzollern had a claim.

The Lutheran Reformation spread through preaching by those educated in the orders of the old religion, who brought their new views to bear on the congregations, both lettered and unlettered, who sat below them. The situation at the Court of Hohenzollern was in some respects exceptional, but there was in other cases a certain absence of definition. In some cases, for instance in Mecklenburg and the Palatinate, the Courts remained Catholic for a time, while the old religion crumbled in the lands about them. In other instances princesses would retain the Catholic Faith which their sons or husbands had relinquished, as did the mother of Philip of Hesse and the sisters of the Duke of Bavaria-Munich. In the case of the sisters, their widowed mother had become a nun and held to the indestructible Catholicism of the House of Austria.[1] At the same time, the children in the coming generation were calmly Lutheran. The presence of the riches of the Church was an argument that played upon the princely cast. Controversy here had little part. There was something sympathetic to the Lutheran spirit in those wide plains of Northern Germany. Those who came within the field of Calvinism were very different.

It was of the nature of Calvinism that it was a religion of the Elect. It was a doctrine that was held with lucid certainty. In the early days of the religion it was grasped by an individual against a hostile atmosphere. There are many examples of this personal

---

[1] These were the sisters of Duke William IV, Sidonia, who was the *fiancée* of Louis V, Elector Palatine and Sibylla, who married him, and Sabina, the wife of Ulrich, Duke of Württemberg, who later separated from her husband. Susanna the youngest married first Casimir, Margrave of Brandenburg-Culmbach and secondly Otto Henry, Count Palatine of Neuburg, who later became Elector Palatine. She died in 1543 the year after he became a Lutheran. This has interest as a set of spreading marriages which henceforth would be confined within denominational barriers.

and fierce change of allegiance. The conversions of the Princesse de Condé, of the French Duchess of Ferrara, and of that Abbess of Jouarre, Charlotte de Montpensier, who became the third wife of William the Silent, all spring to mind. These preliminary comments may help the understanding of Lady Jane.

I

II

Lady Jane Grey

The Marchioness of Dorset had brought up her eldest daughter
for a great position. She herself was a cold-hearted Protestant; life
had gone sour on her. The elder daughter of the Queen of France
and in consequence the senior English niece of Henry VIII, she
had had an unsatisfactory marriage with her cousin Dorset, the
head of the senior line of the Greys. The blood of his stock was
failing, his will was weak. Her last pregnancy, after her two daughters, had produced a dwarf, the Lady Mary. What could be done
with the Lady Jane could only come through her mother's efforts.
It is these, perhaps, that have caused the rather uncharacteristic
portraits of Lady Jane that survive.

The Lady Jane was of course the most eligible heiress in the
kingdom, but the heavy jewellery in the surviving portraits is
clearly that of an important member of the royal family. In the
portrait attributed to Master John, she wears two necklaces and a
large pendant jewel at her breast and six rings upon her fingers.[1]
In her two other portraits,[2] that in the possession of Lord Hastings
and that now destroyed by fire, but formerly belonging to the
Earl of Jersey, she had four rings on the fingers of either hand and
in both pictures an elaborate double necklace of hanging pearls
wound once around the neck.

She was in fact a very small princess, graceful and beautifully
proportioned. Her dark hair had red lights in it. In the portrait
by Master John she has an over-dress of cloth of silver brocade,
which foams delicately over an under-dress of rust-coloured silk.

[1] Now in the National Portrait Gallery, cf. Strong, *Tudor and Jacobean Portraits*, vol. i,
p. 75.
[2] These two portraits are reproduced, *ibid*, vol. i, nos. 147 and 148.

Her sleeves are of a grey lynx fur. She is clasping a pink and holds a pomander chain of antique cameo with a long tassel at the end. She is standing on a Turkey carpet. She has thin fingers on her long slim hand. The whole picture has an air of innocence.

She had a strong judgment, which stood in for knowledge. She was characteristic of one aspect of her period, a young Calvinist princess. She can only be compared with one of the French royal house nine years her senior, the Queen of Navarre.

Lady Jane had one great quality, a burning religious zeal which lit up the character of a rather simple girl. She was in some ways solitary. Had she attained to the Crown of England, it is hard to imagine the ladies of her Court. She was, among other things, a home-trained blue-stocking; she had never travelled. Those who are interested in Lady Jane should visit Bradgate Park for this was the setting, apart from her time in London, for almost the whole of her short life.

Bradgate Park lies with its general outlines quite unchanged at the southern end of that tangled country, which runs up to the limestone rocks of Charnwood Forest. The old brick Tudor house with its terraces and its far-flung walls, built for the most part by the last Marquess of Dorset, has long since lain in ruins. There is much water in the park and the short steep slopes rise up from lakes and streams; it is thickly wooded. It was a rather lonely area and the Marchioness of Dorset hardly dealt with those who were in no sense her equals. The eastern entrance led down to those great level fields which are the heart of Leicestershire.

It is interesting to speculate where Lady Jane developed her taste for study. This certainly did not come from her parents for her father was a nonentity and her mother had a clear understanding of what was otiose and what was useful. It would seem that on the secular side her learning was the fruit of the work of her young tutor, John Aylmer. It was likewise Aylmer who gave publicity to her knowledge and who brought Roger Ascham to visit her at Bradgate. Aylmer, who eventually became Elizabethan Bishop of London and was known for his severity against the Puritans, had been from his youth a *protégé* of Lord Dorset. He came from a family of landowners settled at Aylmer Hall in the Norfolk parish of Tivetshall St Mary; he had been sent to Cambridge by his patron. On graduating he was ordained and became private chaplain at Bradgate Park and tutor to the children there.

He had arrived when Lady Jane was a small child.[1] It is recorded that he taught her 'gently and pleasantly and with fair allurements to learning'. He remained with the family until he was appointed Archdeacon of Stow in Lincolnshire, just before King Edward's death.

Roger Ascham was in all respects a much more significant figure at that time. He was lecturer in Greek at St John's College, Cambridge, and public orator at the University of Cambridge. He was also tutor to the Princess Elizabeth. In the summer of 1550 he visited Bradgate Park on his way to join Sir Richard Moryson, who was leaving for Brussels as ambassador to the Emperor. In his book *The Scholemaster*, first published after his death in 1570, Ascham refers to his first meeting with Lady Jane, who was reading Plato's *Phaedo*, while her family was hunting in the park.[2] She spoke of her parents' severity towards her and contrasts this with Aylmer's gentleness. It seems clear that it was Ascham who drew attention to her learning, to her skill in speaking and writing Greek, and to her knowledge of Hebrew, French and Italian as well as the ancient languages.

The question of her religious approach appears more difficult. Aylmer was certainly an exile for religion at Strasbourg and Zurich under Queen Mary, but in Elizabeth's reign he emerged as a right-wing Anglican, in some ways a precursor of Archbishop Laud. Lady Jane herself developed a close correspondence with Johann Heinrich Bullinger of Zurich, with whom it appears that she had been put in touch by John ab Ulmis, one of his disciples who had come to England and was to some extent under Lord Dorset's protection. There are three of Lady Jane's letters to Bullinger in the Zurich Library. Although the relations between Bullinger and Calvin were often strained, they can between them be regarded as the founders of the Helvetic Confession. Genevan is, perhaps, the best word to describe Lady Jane's Religious Faith.

We shall see in time that it was not the literary education, but

---

[1] The date is uncertain, but it was probably about 1543 when Aylmer was aged twenty-three.
[2] Cf. *The Scholemaster*, ed. J. E. B. Mayor (1863), pp. 33 and 213.

the preoccupation with religion that lay at the heart of Lady Jane Grey's character. In comparison with this great matter, the external events of her career appear to have been of small importance. At King Edward's accession, when she was just nine years old, the Duke of Somerset had looked out upon the situation. He had decided that the King should later marry the second of his five surviving daughters, Lady Jane Seymour. She was a small child; there was no hurry. His son the Earl of Hertford should marry Lady Jane Grey; he was two years her junior.

His brother, Lord Seymour of Sudeley had, as has been explained, another project. He obtained the guardianship of Lady Jane from the Dorsets and undertook in time to arrange a marriage with the young King. It was clear that this would only come about after he had had a successful quarrel with his elder brother. In fact he failed and Lady Jane returned to her father's house. When the whole Seymour system had gone down it was clear that Lord Hertford's chances had disappeared. Lady Jane's *rôle* in all this was wholly passive.

What really mattered was Lady Jane's own situation. She had a burning desire to testify to the Truth, by which she meant the doctrines of Revealed religion. It was this which linked her with her young sovereign. It was their twin deep intensity that soldered them. Among their own contemporaries they were both very much alone. When the key rulers of England are considered, it was only the Duke of Somerset who had shared this concern and he had many other things to think about. More than the King it seems that Lady Jane saw the issues in black and white. Worldly wisdom meant very little to her. Thus her view of the Duke of Northumberland was not one which would commend itself to the ruling circle. To her the Duke was merely a great hypocrite. This was not a good beginning for her relations with the high lord who would be her chief supporter.

The financial prospects of Lady Jane had changed considerably for the better in the last eighteen months of Edward's reign. By the death at Buckden of the sweating sickness of the two young brothers, successively Dukes of Suffolk, the whole Brandon properties had been brought to their half-sister Lady Dorset. She thus inherited Suffolk House, which had formerly been the residence of the Bishop of Norwich, and gave up Dorset Place in Whitehall, which had been the Greys' town house.

At the same time she and her husband set about re-building the former Carthusian priory of Sheen. This had been granted to the Dorsets in 1551 after the attainder of the Duke of Somerset. It was almost opposite across the river from the former Brigettine priory of Sion, which Northumberland had received from the same source.

The dukedom of Suffolk had become extinct, but a new peerage with that title was conferred on Dorset *jure uxoris*, on 4 October 1551. As the new Duke of Suffolk had no male heir, his eldest daughter would have had a great inheritance, even though Bradgate and the Dorset lands would pass eventually to Lord Thomas Grey, the new Duke's brother.

The pieces are now set for the last moves. It may be noticed that the Northumberlands and Suffolks both preferred the fresh airs of the river towards Richmond to the crowded heat of the capital in the summer months.

III

The King's Last Days

Edward VI was now approaching the close of his short reign. In the last months before his illness overtook him he had shown increased activity. In the middle of July 1552, the King set out on the only royal progress which he lived to make. He was accompanied by nine councillors and attended by a bodyguard of just under one hundred and fifty men. He had not hitherto travelled further than thirty miles from London. The Duke of Northumberland was in the North.

The royal party rode slowly through the rich South Country, going from Guildford by way of Petworth, Cowdray, Halnaker and Havant and reaching Portsmouth on 8 August. From that seaport town he moved forward to Southampton, Titchfield and Beaulieu. The farthest point to which he ever reached was Sir Edward Willoughby's house in the east of Dorset. He then came home again by Salisbury and Wilton, Basing and Reading, until he reached Windsor Castle in mid-September.

His character had developed in various ways. Northumberland had given him a kingly pleasure in hunting. He was now more aware of his clothes; he ordered for instance a deep purple cloak. He was still shy. His courtiers seem to have appeared to him as individuals, he never had a sense of the family unit. He was still interested in coinage and in military defence. He had plans for re-developing the organs of his Government. He had still only a single friend, Barnaby Fitzpatrick.

Historians in general have assumed that the idea of Lady Jane's succession began with Northumberland. Professor Jordan in his new book suggests that the first motion was made by the King and that in this the Duke had followed him.[1] It is common ground that this solution appeared to the King as the only way to save that Protestant religion which he was bequeathing to his people. It seems probable that this solution was already present in the germ as soon as the King fell ill with the onset of tuberculosis in the course of January 1553.[2]

On this assumption it seems that the winter months were employed by Northumberland in considering the various aspects of the situation. It was not a well-contrived project and there was no one to help him with advice. He looked for support to too narrow a range of influence. He was always over-confident that he could bend his fellow nobles to his will.

As soon as the Duke of Northumberland decided that Lady Jane should be the inheritrix of the throne, he set about according to the customs of that day to strengthen the position of her immediate relatives. He had decided that she should marry his son Lord Guildford. There remained at his immediate disposal her next sister, Lady Catherine Grey and his own unmarried daughter, Lady Catherine Dudley. The most important of the various pawns was Catherine Grey, for she was the heiress-presumptive to the Queen-designate. There were certain of the great peers who were not available either because their heirs were children or in some cases already married. The man whose support he hoped to buy was the Earl of Pembroke.

The first Earl of Pembroke of the second creation was a man of courage and strength of character, who had built up his own great fortune. In consequence, he was one of the few of the high lords who did not fear Northumberland. He seems, indeed, to have had a respect for his achievement, although he did not particularly admire his judgment. He was ready to support him as long as he politically remained afloat. More could not be asked for in that hard time. His fortune had been made by his marriage to Anne Parr, the sister of Queen Catherine. He had in one respect a strange consistency. From the last years of King Henry's reign he remained at heart politically a Protestant; but there was a difficulty. Lord Pembroke was in no sense pious and, in particular, he

---

[1] *Edward VI: the Threshold of Power.*
[2] For a discussion of this matter of the King's health, cf. Jordan, *op. cit.*, pp. 510–13.

did not like that high-toned Reformation brand of piety which the Grey family represented.

He did not see the English scene as the sanguine Duke would see it. His first wife, probably as the result of her clear Protestantism, was apparently one of the few women friends of Edward VI. At any rate she is the only lady whose death is mentioned in the young King's diary.[1] At this time Pembroke had just re-married one of the daughters of the great House of Talbot, a younger step-sister of the Earl of Shrewsbury. Lady Anne was the widow of the youthful Peter Compton of Compton Winyates. Pembroke knew very well what different 'worlds' were thinking.

What we know of him is coloured by the comments of John Aubrey, who preserved the legend that survived in Wiltshire after a century. Pembroke was represented as a *novus homo* because he was new to Wiltshire.[1] He was in fact the son of Sir Richard Herbert of Ewyas, a man in a respectable position, who was himself a natural child of the first Earl of Pembroke of the first creation. 'He,' wrote Aubrey, 'being a stranger in our country and an up-start, was much envied. . . . He could neither write, nor read, but had a stamp for his name. He was of good natural, but very cholerique. He was strong, set, but bony, (his hair was) reddish favoured.'[2] One thing no man could deny was his sharp native intelligence.

For his own daughter Northumberland decided on an alliance with one of the Protestants among the greater peers, to someone to whom the religious approach of the Greys would prove congenial. There were two names which would come to mind, the Marquess of Northampton and the Earl of Huntingdon; but Northampton was childless, so Catherine Dudley was betrothed to the young Lord Hastings, who was Huntingdon's heir.

It was a difficulty that both these future peers were very youthful, but Hastings was certainly a strong-minded Puritan, brought up to this form of Faith. In later life he would be for many years the Elizabethan Lord President of the North.

All three marriages took place in what had formerly been the Bishop of Norwich's private chapel in Suffolk House. The marriage

[1] Entry under 20 February 1552, *Chronicle*, p. 112.
[2] *Aubrey's Brief Lives*, ed. Oliver Lawson Dick, pp. 141, 142.

of Lady Jane was celebrated first on 26 April 1553, while those of her sister and her sister-in-law took place some six days later. Provision was made from the royal wardrobe of jewels and dresses which had belonged to the attainted Duchess of Somerset for these great ceremonies. At the same time, the Duke of Suffolk's youngest child, the Lady Mary, was affianced to the boy son and heir of Lord Grey de Wilton.

Lord Hastings was about seventeen years of age and his union with Catherine Dudley endured throughout his life. It seems that Lord Herbert was one year younger. In this case his father, a long-sighted man, took care that his marriage was not consummated. It seems that he did not care that his heir should be linked permanently with the Grey family.

The Duke of Northumberland then settled down to secure support for his project for the inheritance of the Crown. The first plan had been to limit the succession to the Lady Jane's heirs male; but it soon became apparent that the King's health would not last out so long. Lady Jane's name was then inserted as the heiress in the document that was drawn up. There are two aspects of this situation. As long as the Duke was forcing his ideas upon a willing sovereign, his actions all made sense.

He had brought Edward down to Greenwich Palace to help his health and his task became simpler, once it had been decided that the Crown should pass to Lady Jane. The dying King had a single wish, adhered to feverishly, that the Crown of England should continue to protect the Word of God. The Duke had little confidence in Archbishop Cranmer; but the King was ready to upbraid the Primate, who surely would not allow the Church of England to pass away from that True and Reformed faith, which together they had built up. Sir Edward Montague made some objections, but these were over-ruled. The King's new settlement would be placed before the Houses of Parliament, when they should meet.

So far it is a simple story and the dying King was then brought back to Whitehall. Northumberland's subsequent actions in getting so many signatures to the 'Devise', as the King's document was called, makes little sense. Peers were brought up from the country, like Westmorland and Worcester, others who could not come sent up their sons, like Bath and Derby. For days the Duke's representatives went on collecting signatures, the Lord Mayor and the alderman, the whole *posse* of judges, the country peers, the knights of the privy chamber.[1] It can hardly be that he trusted that these men would abide by their signatures. Why did he do it? For what really mattered was the great lords of the Council, who had supported the Duke during the King's minority.

But Edward was by this time far from all this tedious detail, the matters of this world were fading from him. His tuberculosis was gaining fast as he now lay dying in his father's palace. He knew well that he had been a virtuous prince, who had spent his whole life in defending the True Reformed religion. He was a solemn child. He savoured sermons which, Sunday by Sunday, had laid before him, well-spiced with flattery, the duties of a Christian ruler. In some ways he was perhaps retarded. His whole life had been spent in innocence; now he would pass on his guardianship of Reformation values to a princess whose life was given to the study of the pure doctrine. The top-hamper of the Romish views of Purgatory had perished. He knew that the pains of his complicated illness were by this time over. Now he stood before the Throne of Grace; he knew that he was due to enter at the Gates of Paradise. He died at nine o'clock in the evening of Thursday, 6 July 1553, a little earlier than had been expected.

The King's death had not been announced and it was only on the third day, 9 July, that Northumberland's daughter, Lady Mary Sidney, fetched Lady Jane from Chelsea Place to Sion. It was then that she learned of that burden of honour that the young King had designed for her. There first came to her the Marquess of Northampton and the Earls of Arundel, Huntingdon and Pembroke, who bent the knee before their sovereign lady. They were followed by the Duchesses of Suffolk and Northumberland. Later there entered the Duke himself who, as President of the Council, told her of the King's decision. The lords then knelt before her and swore by their souls to shed their blood and lose their lives to maintain the just rights of their new sovereign.

---

[1] Among those who did not sign the 'devise' were some North Country peers, the Earl of Cumberland, Lords Dacres of the North, Latimer and Wharton and four peers from the Home Counties, Lords Morley, Mordaunt, Windsor and Vaux of Harrowden.

She was told that the next day she must proceed to take possession of her palace and the Tower. She left Sion in the late morning
and stopped at Durham House, where she dined and robed herself. The weather was warm and sunny as she entered the State
barge and went downstream to the broad steps of the Tower of
London, where she landed at three o'clock in the afternoon. She
wore a white coif with jewels in her hair and a green dress stamped
with gold, with hanging sleeves. This was the last journey that she
ever made.

She walked in procession beneath a canopy to the great hall.
The Duchess of Suffolk carried her daughter's train. In recent
years her weight had increased; she was a low woman with wide
shoulders and a great broad countenance, on the whole rather like
the Queen of Spades. She had come to resemble her uncle, Henry
VIII, and like him her countenance could be inscrutable. Because
of her subsequent line of action, it is worthwhile to try and reach
to her ideas. When she was Marchioness of Dorset before her
grandeurs came upon her, she had paid three visits with her
daughters to the Lady Mary. That princess, who had a faithful
heart, had always felt a gratitude to her aunt the Queen of France,
Lady Dorset's mother. She had been kind to her own mother, and
perhaps what was more to the point had had a strong dislike for
her supplanter Anne Boleyn, then Marchioness of Pembroke. She
had in fact died before Queen Anne's coronation. As to the Duke
of Northumberland, all knew that he lived in a world of men, he
never consulted any woman. This is sufficient to introduce a note
of hesitation in the Duchess of Suffolk's approach to this whole
story.

If it was strange that Lady Dorset should have been Lady Jane's
train bearer, it must be said that it could not have been easy to
find ladies of honour; but this was a matter which lay outside the
scope of the Duke's interests.

He had established Lady Jane in a royal residence[1] where certainly she would be well protected. Apart from members of the
Council, men could not get at her. He would tune the pulpits on

---

[1] The only modern study of this subject is *Lady Jane Grey* by Hester Chapman (1962).
This author agrees with my judgment as to Lady Jane's religious approach, but
attributes to her a much greater ability than I can discern.

her behalf. For himself, the Duke had full command of all the armed forces in the kingdom. In the general field there was only one person who might cause trouble. It would certainly be a great relief to have the Lady Mary safe under lock and key.

IV

The Tower: A Palace

The palace in the Tower of London had been used by the English
sovereigns upon occasion, thus Edward VI had stayed there for a
few days immediately before his coronation. The State Rooms in
the Tower were decorated with the overflow from the other royal
palaces, with tapestries and velvets brought from Genoa. There
were Oriental silks upon the flooring and brocades, both Venetian
and Florentine, upon the walls. There was inevitably a certain lack
of space. In the evenings Lady Jane ate in the private royal dining-
room. She had a canopy above her head. On her right sat the
Duke of Northumberland and on her left the Duke of Suffolk.
Across the table the two Duchesses sat side by side. These were
both strong-minded ladies and deeply antipathetic to one another.
The meals had not the *recherché* quality of those produced from a
royal kitchen; the residents of the Tower were all accustomed to
simpler fare. The news from the outside world was not encouraging, the evenings grim.

The supper over, the two Dukes and their wives went down to
where the barges waited at the royal landing stage. The lanterns
at their bows shone out across the dark, still waters. They moved
off rapidly with practised rowers. It is not difficult to imagine the
impressions of their four passengers as they were rowed quietly up
the stream, the river flowing past them almost noiselessly in the
warm July night. They were put down at the water-steps of their
two palaces at Sheen and Sion.

Lady Jane remained alone. The Tower was not a very healthy
place and hardly cheerful. Drains emptied out into the little
stream which trickled southward under the western drawbridge
until it reached the London river. There were already difficulties

with Lady Jane's young husband. The girl had not surprisingly a tone now of authority and this went with a rather high-pitched note of piety. Lord Guildford appears at this time to have been about nineteen. He was his mother's sixth son, a younger brother and three sisters had died in childhood. It seems that the Duchess was much attached to him. He was a tall slender boy with corn-coloured hair.

He asked his wife that he should be king-consort, but she replied that this depended partly on her own decision and partly on Parliament. But neither House was then in session. He had been brought up by an affectionate father, who had a cheerful liking for all his sons when they proved soldierly. His new marriage had brought to him his first experience of Reformation piety, such was not to be found in the Dudley household.

The Duchess suggested that Lord Guildford should leave the Queen and return with her to Sion House. This might have served to save the poor boy's life, but the Councillors were against it. The men consulted, who were the Earls of Arundel and Pembroke, knew well the Duke's thought about this matter.

From the very beginning there had been anxiety. The Lady Mary had disappeared. As soon as the King was dead, a letter had been despatched to her at Hunsdon stating that her brother was very ill and earnestly desired the comfort of her presence. She set out for the capital and it seems that on reaching Hoddesdon on the London road, she was met by a messenger who told her that Edward was dead.[1] She moved quickly and after a night at Sawston and another at Kenninghall, established herself at Framlingham Castle, one of the possessions of the attainted Duke of Norfolk, which had been granted to her.

The Duke of Northumberland had always been most cheerful in his dealings with the holders of the great satrapies. He had not taken the title of Lord Protector, nor had he, unlike Somerset, adopted the designation of 'His Highness'. On the other hand, he was a very soldierly man; he inspired fear. In the long course of Tudor history there was no other time when the great noblemen

[1] This is described as a member of the Throckmorton family supported by her London goldsmith. There seems to be some doubt about the identity of this messenger.

were so inscrutable as in those difficult days which followed on Edward's death.

When morning broke, the two Secretaries of State came to the Tower to attend on Lady Jane. Sir William Petre, who was staying at his house in Aldersgate, was still a stranger to her. She could not gain much comfort from that cold closed visage. The other Secretary was very different. She had been familiar all her life with Sir John Cheke, the Cambridge scholar. He was only twenty-nine and had spent all his life in Cambridge, he belonged to a merchant's family living over against the Market Cross and his mother still kept a wine shop in the town. He had had a very distinguished academic career. He had been public orator to the university and was now the non-resident provost of King's College. He was a devoted Protestant. He knew little of England apart from the university; he thought that Englishmen would welcome a scholar queen.

Soon the news came through of Lady Mary's movements. She was now settled at Framlingham and had set up her standard there. She had been proclaimed queen at Norwich. The gentry of East Anglia were riding in to her support. As a *riposte*, a proclamation was sent out composed by Cheke and signed by Lady Jane. The one that went to the Marquess of Northampton has been preserved. 'You will,' it runs, 'endeavour yourself in all things to the uttermost of your power, not only to defend our just title [to the Crown], but also assist us to disturb, repel and resist, the feigned and untrue claim of the Lady Mary, bastard daughter to our great-uncle Henry the Eighth of famous memory.' If one thinks over the situation, one impression seems inescapable. The Lady Jane was beautifully educated and very learned, but was she at all intelligent? After the proclamation she grew sick of a fever and for a few days could take no action.

The Lady Mary's letter, sent from Kenninghall on her journey, soon reached the Council. There were few peers resident in East Anglia and the dukedom of Norfolk was under attainder. The second Earl of Sussex, a member of the Howard affinity, and the Earl of Bath, who now lived with his third wife at Hengrave Hall, had both joined the Lady Mary. The Earl of Oxford stayed quietly at his home at Castle Hedingham.

The Duke of Northumberland called a meeting of the Council
and they all assembled at the Tower of London. The Archbishop's
barge brought Cranmer down from Lambeth; the two Dukes
came downstream from Sheen and Sion; Lord Pembroke came
across from Baynard's Castle. The rest rode through the crowded
City streets. The day was fresh and still; it was lovely July weather.
Northumberland knew well what he required. The letter that he
wished them all to sign was passed round fair and clear. 'Madam,'
it ran, 'we have received your letters of the 9th of this instant,
declaring your supposed title . . . to the Imperial Crown of this
Realm, and all the Dominions thereunto belonging. For answer
whereof, this is to advertise, that for as much as our sovereign
Lady, Queen Jane is after the death of our sovereign Lord Edward
the Sixth, invested and possessed with a just and right title in the
Imperial Crown of this Realm, not only by good order of ancient
laws of this Realm, but also by our late sovereign Lord's letters
patent, signed with his own hand and sealed with the Great Seal
of England, in presence of the most part of the nobles, councillors,
judges, with divers other grave and sage personages, assenting and
subscribing to the same.' So far it was a rotund and stately document, but now it grew a little sharper. 'We must therefore,' it
went on, 'of most bounden duty and allegiance assent unto her said
Grace, and to none other, except we should, which faithful subjects cannot, fall into grievous and unspeakable enormities.'

There then came a somewhat tedious recital of the divorce made
between 'the King of famous memory' Henry VIII and the Lady
Catherine, and the Lady Mary was required to show herself 'quiet
and obedient'.

All those around the table quietly signed: the Archbishop of
Canterbury and the Bishop of Ely, the Lord Chancellor, the Duke
of Suffolk, the Marquesses of Winchester and Northampton, the
Earls of Arundel, Bedford, Huntingdon, Pembroke and Shrewsbury, Lords Cobham, Rich and Darcy of Chiche, who held the
office of Lord Chamberlain. There was also a small number of
officials. The Duke of Northumberland's eye was on them all.

As they sat in the constricted space of that high room with those
damp-sodden walls, the 'weeping' walls of the old Tower, there
was one thing which united them; they were all men of great

K

possessions. There they sat serious and inscrutable. What the Duke of Northumberland thought as he saw their easy signatures we shall never know. He was a *condottiere*, a man of straightforward values. This was not like the Elizabethan world which had at its disposal an army of spies and agents, men who would haunt the kitchens or hide behind the arras in the withdrawing rooms of their noble friends. Northumberland had no such means of knowledge.

To each of the great men the situation was dangerous, but very simple. Had the Lady Mary continued on her journey to the capital, she would by now have been locked up within the Tower and Northumberland's dominion would have continued. This would also have been the case if she had fled overseas to her cousin, the Emperor in the Low Countries. But in fact she was at liberty, an unknown factor. Northumberland controlled the only troops immediately available. If there was an *émeute*, any of these high personages might well be killed.

One cannot tell how many of them communicated secretly with the Lady Mary, for naturally the documentation has not survived. But judging by her later action it is evident that several must have done so. It was easy for a trusted servant to ride out across Essex to where the Royal Standard of England fluttered in the July weather above the walls of Framlingham.

Meanwhile, the life went on unchanging in the Tower of London. The day following the Council meeting the Marquess of Winchester came in to Lady Jane. He had been simply Lord St John of Basing when Northumberland took over power and through him he had been raised to an earldom and a marquessate. He had also received the office of Lord Treasurer of England. He was a careful man, quite remote in temperament from the Duke, but he would support him so long as the political climate should remain fair weather. He had not favoured the Grey succession; for different reasons both the Duke and the Duchess of Suffolk were uncongenial to him. Sentimentality had naturally no place in the thought of public men. There was no trace of sentiment in what must be the future fate of Lady Jane. He performed the necessary duties of his great office.

He waited upon Lady Jane and brought her articles of jewellery deposited in boxes and casquets in the Jewel House in the Tower, which had belonged to the six queens, who had been the wives of the old sovereign.[1] These included a golden fish and an ornament in the form of a lizard in white silver. There were tablets of gold, one with a white sapphire and another with the image of Our Lady of Pity engraved on a blue stone. There were buttons of gold and many pearls, a pair of bracelets set with jacynths and orange-coloured amethysts. There were big golden buttons, each set with six seed pearls, and also thirteen table diamonds. Our Lady of Pity would have meant little to the young girl; but all the same it was a disquieting gift, these broken trinkets of the six dead queens.

However, there were more cheerful things to think about. On the same day she gave instructions to her new brother-in-law Lord Ambrose Dudley, who was now Keeper of the Palace of the Tower. Orders were sent for twenty yards of purple velvet, twenty-five of Holland cloth and twenty-three of coarser lining to make the robes for the new Queen 'against her removal from the Tower'.

[1] This inventory is to be found among the Harleian MSS, no. 611.

V

The Northern Progress

At a meeting of the Council at the Tower it was decided that the Duke should go north to deal with the supporters of the Lady Mary. It was a difficult choice to have to make, but there was no alternative. There was no other nobleman, among the true supporters of Lady Jane, who had the qualities of a soldier. The news that came from up and down the country was most discouraging. It was reported credibly that the Earl of Derby had declared himself in favour of the Lady Mary and was marching towards London in her support. A body of local men had gathered in Buckinghamshire under Lord Windsor and Sir Edward Hastings, who was Lord Huntingdon's Catholic brother. The Earl of Oxford had left Castle Hedingham and had gone to Framlingham. None of these episodes was of real importance, but they showed the way the wind was blowing.

On Friday, 14 July, the Duke of Northumberland rode forth at the head of a body of six hundred men with a train of guns. Lords Clinton, Grey de Wilton, Huntingdon, and Westmorland bore him company and his officers included his three sons, the Earl of Warwick, Lord Ambrose, and Lord Robert. Lord Guildford was left behind them in the Tower. The day before 'three great carts[1] full of all manner of ordnance, great guns and small, spears, arrows and gunpowder' had been brought into the fortress.

The Lady Jane was now very lonely. In another section of the Tower there lodged the prisoners, the old Duke of Norfolk, the Duchess of Somerset and Bishops Gardiner and Bonner. They were all waiting anxiously for her disaster. It was not that they had any feeling about the Grey family. It was Northumberland

[1] Machyyn's *Diary*, p. 36.

for whose blood they hungered. The Duchess of Somerset was one of the first generation of women among the Gospellers. She was a failed conspirator and, as far as the Duke was concerned, she had a pure unsleeping hatred. Lady Jane's only companion was Lord Guildford. (In another portion of the fortress there was kept the captive lion. One hopes that he was fed with regularity in these rough days.)

In the royal quarters of the Tower there was heaped up a mass of odds and ends of jewellery, a muffler of purple velvet embroidered with pearls, and a bejewelled muffler of sable skin, set with emeralds, rubies and turquoises.[1] There was a hat of purple velvet, pearl-embroidered, and a cap of black velvet which was set with a square table ruby. There was a shirt with golden ruffles and another of gold colour which was stitched with red and silver silk. There were six clocks. One was a fair striking clock standing upon a mine of silver, and there was a little one which also struck, within a case of 'latten', book fashion, engraved with a rose crowned, and the motto *Dieu et mon droit*.

There was a picture of the Duchess of Suffolk in a gold box and another of Queen Catherine Parr 'that is deceased'. There was a dog-collar wrought in red leather with gold bells. There were also some possessions of Lord Guildford's, a 'sword grille' of red silk and gold and a white doublet and hose of silk and velvet. These were the tattered ends of all her glory.

Meanwhile the Duke pressed northwards towards Cambridge. Riding on ahead of his troops, he reached the university city about midnight. Northampton, Huntingdon and his three sons joined him there. The other peers, who had started with him, had now detached themselves. He then marched his men to Bury St Edmunds, but on the way many deserted him. He returned to Cambridge, where he stayed at Trinity College with Dr Sandys. An unsuccessful soldier, he must have been a grim visitor in that quiet place. There he heard of the action of the Councillors in London, which he might well have foreseen to be inevitable.

He had left the Duke of Suffolk in command at the Tower and on the Sunday there was news of a body of ten thousand men, supporters of the Lady Mary, who had assembled at Drayton and,

[1] These details are preserved among the Hatfield MSS.

under the command of Lord Paget, were now marching on the capital. It is not suggested that this was a real military threat, but Northumberland had left with all his soldiers.

On the next day the Councillors met at the Tower and then asked Suffolk's permission for a transfer of their meeting to Baynard's Castle, which would be more convenient for the Imperial and the French ambassadors, who sought for audience. There they decided quite unanimously to support Queen Mary. This may have been a plan long matured, probably originating with the Earl of Pembroke. It was decided that Pembroke and Arundel should go to Framlingham taking with them the Great Seal. They also brought with them a letter which expressed their new views quite exactly. It is no good changing unless you change completely.

'Our bounden duties,' so runs this document, 'most humbly remembered to your Most Excellent Majesty we . . . have this day proclaimed in your city of London, Your Majesty to be our true and sovereign liege-lady and Queen, most humbly beseeching Your Majesty to pardon and remit our former infirmities, and most graciously to accept our meaning which has ever been to serve Your Highness truly and this shall remain with all our powers and forces to the effusion of our blood.' The conclusion was in keeping. 'Thus we do (declare) and shall daily pray to Almighty God for the preservation of your most royal person long to reign.' This paper was then superscribed. '(Given in) the first year of your most prosperous reign.'

It seems that all the Councillors were present, except for Archbishop Cranmer and the Duke of Suffolk and those who had left with the Duke of Northumberland for Cambridge. The same morning, the Archbishop of Canterbury went to the Tower on his last visit and the Duke of Suffolk hastened to append his signature to this new proclamation. On Tower Hill he proclaimed Queen Mary. The story is well-known of his return to the Tower to find his daughter sitting alone in the Council Chamber under the canopy of State. He told her what had happened and she asked his permission to go home, but this was now impracticable.

The news soon reached the Duke at Cambridge. Affairs might have been different if he had chosen the Lady Elizabeth. Now his support had crumbled all about him. He might still have saved himself. He had the money with him to pay the soldiers. With a selected band of troops to guard him on his journey, he might have made his way northward on the road which crossed the Isle of Ely and then ridden up through the cathedral city and down to King's Lynn across the Fens. There were plenty of Protestants within King's Lynn and he would have a good sum to offer to some merchant captain, who would embark him and sail along the coast of Norfolk and then down the North Sea to land at some French port, perhaps Le Havre. There were various reasons why this did not happen. Perhaps Northumberland did not trust Henry II of France, when it came to dealing with a defeated ally. However, in fact, he made no such effort.

Instead he went out into the Market Place and called his secretary to fill his cap for him. He threw up his cap and shouted in a hollow voice, 'God save Queen Mary'. The gold coins fell and shone upon the paving stones. His day was over.

VI

The Tower: A Prison

Very shortly after he had proclaimed Queen Mary, the Duke had been arrested. There is one reference to Northumberland on his last journey. It was reported that on the evening of his arrest, the Duke was seen still wearing his red cloak as he and Sir John Gates rode strongly guarded, towards London in the heavy rain. The next day, he reached his destination. The roses were in flower in the Queen's garden in the Tower.

From the moment of his arrival it was clear to him that his life was almost over. He had made, without much hope, a suggestion to the Earl of Arundel that the Queen might allow him to live in peace. He must have known that this was quite impossible.

Three of his sons were in prison with him and there was a small assortment of his noble supporters. In the first place there was the Duke of Suffolk. Both dukes had publicly proclaimed Queen Mary at the end, but it could not be forgotten that Suffolk was the father of the young Pretender. For the rest, there were those men of standing who had not been present at the Council when the Earl of Pembroke had swung that body to support Queen Mary. Lord Huntingdon, for instance, had gone north with the Duke in his attempt to capture the Lady Mary, as also had the Marquess of Northampton.

Cranmer and Latimer were still at liberty, but Nicholas Ridley was already in the Tower. He had gone to Framlingham to submit himself to the new Queen, but had been repulsed. One of her first actions had been to restore Edmund Bonner to the see of London. Northumberland was now in that nest of towers which contained the prisoners in the great citadel and these men were now his new companions.

In many aspects the Tower has changed. The greater part of
the palace buildings have been taken down, as have the Wardrobe
and Lanthorn Towers, as also those two circular slender towers
then called Coldharbour, which stood between the White Tower
and the river. The wide moat is now dry. The Lion Gate has also
vanished; it then led to the Lion Tower which at that time had a
separate moat around it. The menagerie of wild animals at this
point has long since been removed. There was at that time a cub
to which a lioness gave birth in 1551. It long survived its human
companions, who were prisoners like itself.

The Lion, Middle and Bayward Towers led into the fortress
from the only entrance, apart from the Water Gate. This was the
way leading from the City. The Garden Tower and the Beauchamp Tower formed together a single block. The privilege of
walking on the leads was sometimes given, but it was very seldom
that this was extended to those high open pathways like that between the Beauchamp and Curfew Towers. It was not desirable
that prisoners should find themselves out of sight of their warders.
The height of these towers should not be over-emphasized. Thus
the Garden (or Bloody) Tower was a building of three storeys with
an elevation of only forty-seven feet.[1]

Eastwards a stone-flagged court, bordered by sycamores, led out
towards the Iron Gate from which admittance could be gained to
Little Tower Hill, but this entrance was never opened. The series of
defences was very intricate. The most unchanged of the surviving
buildings is the exterior of the White Tower, that great Keep
which dates from the later part of the reign of William the Con-
queror. Its four towers still stand above its curtain wall. Their
turrets were of lead and above them rose the gilded vanes. The
interior contained the chapel of St John with its squat Norman
pillars suggestive of the Lady Chapel, built at the same date in the
cathedral at Durham. In the reign of Edward VI the frescoes had
been covered with whitewash and the stained glass had been
removed.

It is not surprising that beauty only came to the Tower of
London on moonlit nights in the summer weather. Then the high
white-washed walls of the White Tower shone in the darkness

[1] Called since the seventeenth century the Bloody Tower.

and moonlight fell on the wide waters of the moat, as the tides rose and fell on the London river. Night time was quiet. Men did not escape, or even seek to escape, from those strong walls.

The Bell Tower, which was sixty feet in height, carried a bell hung in a wooden turret on its summit. According to regulations made in 1607, and probably part of an established practice, 'When the Tower bell doth ring at nights for the shutting in of the gates, all the prisoners, with their servants, are to withdraw themselves into their chambers, and not to goe forth that night.'[1] This bell was also used as a general warning for the whole fortress.

The Tower was honeycombed by secret passages and there were hidden alcoves which could be used as listening posts at selected points throughout the prison. There were variations in the accommodation depending upon the rank of the great prisoners. The life was in some ways fairly tolerable for those of the highest station. Thus the Duchess of Somerset had had her own attendants and these were likewise granted to Lady Jane. The Dukes of Northumberland and Suffolk also gained by the arrangements that had been made for the old Duke of Norfolk in the last reign.

Curiously enough the first leader to be brought to trial was Lord Northampton. It was true that, unlike most other peers, he had been a genuine supporter of Lady Jane, whose religious faith he shared. For the rest he was in fact almost a cipher. He had been Captain of the Yeomen of the Guard and at the end, Lord Chamberlain. He held the lord lieutenantcy of the counties of the Eastern Midlands, Cambridgeshire, Bedfordshire, Huntingdon and Northampton. He also held the same post in Norfolk. It appears that it was decided that these offices should now be rendered vacant and this secured for him his early trial. On 13 August he was condemned to death. At the same time, he was deprived of his marquessate and his other peerages. Lord Hereford claimed all the lands which had come to him from the Bohuns, Earls of Essex. Northampton also lost the Order of the Garter. Four days later Northumberland was brought up and condemned.

[1] Cf. Lord Ronald Leveson-Gower, *The Tower of London*, i. p. 29.

VII

Queen Mary's Judgment

Queen Mary always retained an admiration for her great father.
With her deep voice, a certain quality of heartiness and her clear-
cut views, she had in some ways a resemblance to him. She was
more unmistakably her father's daughter than was her step-sister
Queen Elizabeth. In the latter case there was a synthetic element
in all that *rôle*.

It was a result of her sharp, well-founded judgments that the
Duke of Northumberland could have no hopes from her. In her
view the Duke was the *fons et origo* of all the trouble. She would
not be harsh towards the Duke's children and she had a real
understanding of the nature of his authority over the other members of the Privy Council. She had in an unsentimental fashion a
quality of mercy in her dealings with the great lords.

There was first of all the Hastings family. Lord Huntingdon
was in the Tower, but he was soon set free. He received from the
Queen authority which he used faithfully. Curiously enough, she
never seems to have minded much about the religion of the rich.
Later in her reign, the position of this house was buttressed, when
Cardinal Pole, who was Lady Huntingdon's uncle, came over as
Archbishop of Canterbury.

The Earl of Pembroke quickly found favour. Perhaps the Henrican quality, in the political sense, in his outlook and his career
drew the Queen to him. At no time did she ever think that he was
a Roman Catholic. She understood his carefulness for his new
great family. She explained to him that it could not help the
Herberts to retain their association with the Greys. The marriage
of Lord Herbert with Lady Catherine Grey was dissolved very
quickly as *matrimonium ratum sed non consummatum*.

The most remarkable case of all was that of the Duchess of Suffolk. She was received in audience as soon as the Queen reached London. She secured the release of her husband from the Tower. Thereafter she was always prominent at Queen Mary's Court; her younger daughters, Lady Catherine and Lady Mary were ladies of honour. There was never any change in the indefectible Protestantism which marked this family. The Queen herself did not expect it. Besides, the Queen had always a feeling for anyone who reflected her father's image; perhaps this was what she saw in the Duchess of Suffolk's bold broad countenance.

Queen Mary never troubled any member of the Council who signed the proclamation of her rights which, under Pembroke, it had drawn up, for example, there is the curious case of the Bishop of Ely. Thomas Goodrich is one of the most obscure figures of this period. He was one of the first bishops to be consecrated by Dr Cranmer and had followed quite exactly all Henry VIII's ideas. He had later commended himself to Northumberland, who had raised him to the lord chancellorship on the resignation of Lord Rich, in the first days of 1552. On Queen Mary's accession he resigned the Great Seal, but he was left undisturbed in the bishopric of Ely and died at Somersham in Huntingdonshire on 10 May 1554, before the formal reconciliation of England with the Holy See. The former support by the councillors for Lady Jane was all forgiven. They were only joined by Bishop Gardiner and Bishop Bonner and Bishop Tunstall.

The Queen's mind was focused on a single object, the destruction of the Duke of Northumberland and with him his two henchmen, Sir John Gates and Sir Thomas Palmer. It was not long before the Queen's judgment became apparent. The frieze of his grand friends passed away, and he was left with his two rough companions. Sir Thomas had the reputation of a man of courage. He had betrayed Somerset to Northumberland, he had cleaved close to him, determined that the Lady Jane would make his fortune. He seems to have acted to some extent as his chief of staff; his mind ran on military *coups*, but these in fact had not proved successful. Sir John was Captain of the King's Guard. They were not cheerful friends for the poor Duke.

At the same time, there were certain compensations. His three sons, Lord Warwick and Lord Ambrose and Lord Robert were all released to join their brother, Lord Henry, who was always free. His wife was busy working hard for them. Further, there seemed some hope for his son, Lord Guildford. He knew that he had compelled this boy into his marriage, but Lady Jane was accommodated in Mr Partridge's house within the Tower. It seemed possible that in time the Queen might pardon her and then Lord Guildford, also, would go free.

It was at this time in his imprisonment that the Duke's thought went back to his religion. Later it was the practice of his Protestant contemporaries, including John Knox, to suggest that the Duke had always been a secret Catholic. This seems to me to be at variance with his open character. He realized that his trial would soon be followed by his execution. He was not by nature religious, but his mind went back quite simply to the doctrines he had been taught as a child.

He had been brought up in the Roman faith. He now went again to Mass and returned to the Sacraments. On the scaffold he made his famous declaration. He was wearing a gown of crane-coloured damask, that is of a silver grey material. He slipped this off and then made his statement. 'Good people,' he began, 'hither I am come this day to die as you know. Through false and seditious preachers I have erred from the Catholic Faith and the true doctrine of Christ. The doctrine I mean which hath continued through all Christendom since Christ. For, good people, there is and has ever been since Christ a Catholic Church, which Church hath continued from Him and His disciples in one unity and concord. More than that, good people, you have in your creed, Credo Ecclesiam Catholicam, which Church is the same Church which hath continued ever since Christ, throughout (all the world) and the apostles, saints and doctors there, and yet doeth as I have said before. Of which I do profess myself to be one, and do steadfastly believe therein. I speak unfeignedly from the bottom of my heart.'[1]

He went back to the old religion very naturally and with complete simplicity. There was no future for him in this world. His

[1] Printed in *England under the reigns of Edward VI and Mary* by Patrick Fraser Tytler quoting the Harleian MSS.

mundane wisdom fell away from him. He turned at once to God as his ancestors had done for many generations.

It is not surprising that his line of argument should greatly have angered Lady Jane. It was something that she had never known. Since childhood she had been educated in the fresh-formed thought of the Reformation. His words were wholly foreign to all the new theology, but the Duke had returned to his first beginnings.

VIII

Epilogue

The final tragedy was the responsibility of the Duke of Suffolk. In any case, the Queen's magnanimity was turning cold. The Marquess of Northampton was pardoned in the course of January. He was now Sir William Parr and almost penniless. Further the private Act of Parliament was repealed which had settled the legitimacy of his second marriage.

Meanwhile, Lady Jane stayed on in Mr Partridge's house. She had had an unhappy life and was at peace. The great fire which warmed the little room blazed up in her dining chamber. The winter rains poured down upon the Tower of London. She was sustained by her burning religious faith. To the little group which gathered round her, she spoke sharp words about the Duke of Northumberland's defection. Her young husband seldom ate now at her table; it seems that he was not at ease with her.

Queen Mary had a low opinion of Lady Jane and this might argue in favour of her survival. Contempt is a prophylactic. All might yet have gone well with her, if she had not been sent to her death by her own father.

It was in the winter of her second year in prison that the Duke of Suffolk was brought into the Tower. He was a man of narrow intellect and this fact was a burden to his wife and would prove lethal to his eldest daughter. At the time of Sir Thomas Wyatt's 'stirs', he had been caught up into rebellion, not against Queen Mary, but against the Spanish Marriage. It seems that the Queen who for good reason distrusted him, ordered Suffolk to go out against the rebels and that he refused. He and his brother, Lord John, both went into the Midlands; they were taken in a cottage of one of their gamekeepers at Astley Cooper in Warwickshire.

Suffolk was brought to London by the Earl of Huntingdon and the Hastings family were now obedient to the Queen of England. The Duke of Suffolk was only just thirteen days within the Tower and then he was beheaded; but even before his execution disaster had overtaken Lady Jane.

It was her misfortune that in her retired life she had had no personal friends and from the angle of politics her cause was dead. The only name that came before the various opponents of the Queen was the Princess Elizabeth. Had Queen Mary had good advice, she would have seen this.

Further, the Lady Jane could gain no help from her only close relative, her mother. The Duchess of Suffolk had in a remarkable degree that common sense which was a Tudor heritage. She had indignation against her husband for his folly and a strong sense of self-preservation. In these weeks she decided that she must, as soon as practicable, make a second marriage with someone whose lack of position would save her from all future trouble. She chose Adrian Stokes, a red-headed boy who was her master of the horse. She would place herself outside the dangerous realm of politics.

The Lady Jane seems to have realized this; she left letters for her father and for her sister, Lady Catherine, none for her mother. The execution was a simple matter, for both Lady Jane and her husband had been found guilty of treason in the previous autumn. On the morning of her death she would not see her husband lest the interview should disturb 'her holy tranquillity'. It seems that in her view she died simply and purely for the Reformed Faith. It was to save this priceless heritage that Edward had bequeathed the Crown to her. It took some time for this fact to be well-understood in England. Her life and death was a subject on which neither Queen Elizabeth nor Cecil, her great minister, would ever dwell.

The Duchess of Northumberland was struck by sorrow. She had never cared very much for her daughter-in-law, but Lord Guildford was always her favourite son. One may perhaps over-stress the importance of the Duke of Suffolk's action; and this is not to exonerate Queen Mary, who bore the full responsibility for the girl's death.

The Tower of London was never again used as a royal palace.

With the beheading of the Duke of Suffolk, the last of those concerned with Northumberland's conspiracy was now removed. The leaders of Sir Thomas Wyatt's 'stir' soon followed them.

As sometimes happens in the tide of politics, the Tower was for once empty of its prisoners, except of course for the lion. The rain came sweeping down; there was no fog in the City in the sixteenth century. The moonlight glittered on the golden vanes of the White Tower. The night came down in silence on the old grim fortress.

Great changes were to come about in Queen Mary's reign. The reconciliation with Rome could be foreseen. It may also be said that the Queen was always loyal to her own supporters. She had a clear understanding of her father's Court. On the other hand it was both unwise and cruel to burn the bishops, Cranmer the Primate and Ridley, Latimer, Hooper and Ferrar his four suffragans, especially since three of them had become prelates in her father's reign; but the real tragedy, which could not have been expected or foreseen, was the creation of the Marian Martyrs.

Her husband, King Philip, was to follow a line of action similar to hers in his attempt to eradicate heresy from the Low Countries. The Queen had never come across the city poor. Her experience of that class was confined to her household servants, all country people of the old religion. The Protestant Martyrs of her reign all came from two allied classes, the lower ranks of the town burgesses and the literate element among the urban poor. They had come to their knowledge of the new religion by a careful reading of the Bible, a study which was full of effort. They had reached to this in the quiet days of the *Pax Edwardiana*. They read those strange names of the Old Testament and the many fascinating stories. They had in their outlook a strain of obstinacy which has always marked the English working class. Why should they give up what their own minds had attained to? These men formed no military danger, they made no plots. The responsibility for the persecution was widely spread; but in the end it must come back to the lonely Queen. I do not imagine that she ever realized what she had done; but nevertheless it was this tragedy, more than any other factor, which prevented the Roman Catholic Church regaining its hold upon the English nation.

L

More than the other members of her great house, Queen Mary always showed a kindness towards her richer subjects. The high stocks were very sparsely represented among those who fled abroad during her reign. The only names that come to mind are those of Katharine Duchess of Suffolk and her second husband, and Lord Russell, who inherited the earldom of Bedford from his father. But what about the religious practice of the many wealthy and non-Roman families, who had helped to seat her on the Throne? This, as far as I am aware, is a question that has not been asked.

I would suggest a partial answer. There was never any compulsion in the Marian world to receive Communion. A clear determination was always present not to expose the Sacred Elements to the risks of sacrilege. Those who had a mild preference for the customs of King Henry's generation would perhaps be not unready to attend the restored Mass. Many of the parish priests had passed through different phases. The Papacy meant nothing to the average men and women of the richer classes at that time. The more they heard of Paul IV, the less appealing would he sound; but for the most part, surely they never gave a thought to him. There is no doubt that the Spanish Marriage was in general unpopular.

The new Queen was most unhappy, the affections of her maturity concentrated on her young husband, while King Philip could only offer the seemly courtesy of his Castilian upbringing. Further, the Queen was ageing and she could not control her sister. She might force Elizabeth to a marriage, but not into the marriage bed. In consequence she could not make an alliance for her from which in time she could not free herself. In many respects it was a time of hiatus. And probably the younger generation went to Church as little as they had ever done since King Henry had thrown down the old religion. If this picture has an approximation to the truth, the Henricans passed through the brief years of Queen Mary's reign with great tranquillity. From this they would emerge to help in the formation of the Church of England as we now know it.

This is at any rate one of the views in which the changes of religion between the death of Henry VIII and the establishment of the Elizabethan Settlement can be envisaged. But one should not neglect to remember the great areas of indifference or, to put it in another way, the fashion in which the religious element was confused with that of the new patriotic nationalism and the pull of secular advantage. And over all, there was the great pull of the State.

It can be said that the Henrican point of view, to use a term which in itself is clumsy, was dominant in 1547 among those peers and courtiers who were unaffected by the new Protestant movement. It seems to me that this was at the root of the outlook of the great majority of the leaders who would come in time to support the Lady Mary. In that very limited sphere, in which specifically religious matters were concerned, it would tend to welcome back King Henry's mass.

It would seem that the idea of Rome itself was uncongenial to the great mass of the leadership of Marian supporters. From the first, it was very clear to them that nothing must be allowed to interfere with the lay holders of monastic land. Let us take a glance at the future for a moment. It may be said that the Henrican grouping accepted listlessly the restoration of the links with Rome; few would then think that these were lasting. We are now considering the ruling classes. It may be suggested, for in such matters there can be no proof, that taken on the whole they were not a sacrament-receiving generation. And then when Queen Elizabeth had reached the throne there came together the now ageing Henrican generation, the young Protestant adventurers and the solid Protestants, who had grown up in King Edward's reign. It seems to me that the Henrican mould was a seed-plot for Catholic doctrine encapsulated in an anti-Roman framework. This with the Protestant doctrinal outlook would later flower in the Church of England.

This is a view of the situation, but it is at best only a surmise. It is hard to attempt to study ways of thought on which the documents are insufficient. At any rate from very different origins, the leaders of the Church of England were brought together; this was a Communion which was inextricably associated with the Queen's position. A constantly increasing patriotism, which that sovereign knew well how to fan, gave confidence to the situation.

It is now the time to speak about the Roman Catholics. The

Old Religion had lasted for many centuries and, however critical the English Government might be of the Papacy, the Pope was always recognized as the Vicar of Christ. There were throughout the South the members of the Catholic minority and also the much larger Catholic proportion in the North, which through this reign remained remote from London politics. At the same time, it was a characteristic of those who lived within reach of the influence of the capital that they were not a persecution-resisting body. As a grouping they did not hold out against the Church Ordinances of Queen Elizabeth.

The Catholic renascence, when it came in the second half of the Elizabethan period, for the most part reclaimed a small part of the former southern flock, gathered the firm Catholicism of Lancashire and the North and made the individual conversions from the universities. This movement of reclamation hardly affected the general position of the Church of England, which was now an amalgam of Protestant and post-Henrican elements, whose spiritual force was strengthened by a national patriotism. Roman Catholicism and Protestantism were both behind the strength of different new Nation States.

Finally, the Duchess of Northumberland spent her last months at Chelsea Manor, dying in that house on 15 January 1555. She lived in quietness and relatively in poverty; she had returned to the practice of the Old Religion. Her days were full of sadness. In addition to her other losses, her son John, Earl of Warwick, had died as soon as he was released from the Tower. These were the first days of the Spanish Marriage and she had called upon Spaniards of high position to help her children. For this reason she bequeathed a green parrot to the Duchess of Alba and a little clock 'with a moon in it' and a watch with the golden number to Don Diego de Mendoza. Her other bequests revealed her new-found poverty. Her manor of Halesowen, which she described as 'my very own land given me by my Lord my dear husband' passed to Lord Ambrose, now her eldest son.

There were certain bequests of dresses, a gown of purple velvet lined with fur and another of black barred velvet lined with sable to her daughters Lady Hastings and Lady Mary Sidney. The green and gold hangings from her gallery went to Sir Henry, the latter's husband.

In the next reign there was a swing of the pendulum in her children's favour. Two of the Duke's sons, Lord Ambrose and Lord Robert became respectively the Earls of Warwick and of Leicester; but there the family ended. The Duke of Northumberland had been borne in on a tide of fortune and in time the tide receded.

APPENDICES

The Portraiture of Northumberland

It is a remarkable fact that among the chief political leaders in the second half of the sixteenth century in England the Duke of Northumberland is alone in leaving no authentic portrait. For many years attention was concentrated on the Penshurst painting. When compiling the volumes of his *Portraits of Illustrious Persons of Great Britain*, which was first published in 1814 by Edmund Lodge, at that time Lancaster herald, he naturally applied to Sir John Shelley Rolls Sidney, Bart, at that time the owner of Penshurst Place. This was the most likely place to find a portrait of the Duke, for when the Duchess died at Chelsea Manor in 1555 and its contents were distributed, Penshurst, the home of Sir Henry Sidney the Duke's favourite son-in-law, was the only great house belonging to the family where a large portrait could be placed. Neither Lord Ambrose nor Lord Robert Dudley had at that time a permanent home. This probability is further supported by the fact that no portrait of the Duke of Northumberland is recorded in the very detailed list of the furniture and portraits at Kenilworth Castle at the time of the death of Lord Robert, then Earl of Leicester.

The portrait at Penshurst was described as by Holbein and Lodge repeated this ascription. Holbein is the painter to whom all the mid-sixteenth century portraits in the country houses of England are attributed; but in fact he died in 1543 before the young Sir John Dudley had reached the circle in which Holbein worked. Further the dress in this portrait is that of a young man of the Elizabethan period.[1]

The Duke of Northumberland does, however, appear in a rather unsubtle anti-Papal caricature issued early in King Edward's reign and now preserved in the National Portrait Gallery.[2] There

[1] 'This portrait cannot be substantiated', R. C. Strong, *Tudor and Jacobean Portraits* (1969), i, p. 235.   [2] Cf. *ibid*, i, pp. 344–5.

appear in this picture representations, they can hardly be called likenesses, of Archbishop Cranmer, the Duke of Somerset and of Northumberland, then Earl of Warwick. These figures are all small. Those of the Archbishop and of Somerset bear no resemblance to their known portraits. There is therefore no reason to suppose that that of Dudley, only identified by his Garter chain, bears any resemblance to the original.

Select Chart Pedigrees

I The Lisle Peerage

II The Parr Connexion

III The Grey Descent

IV The Dukes of Suffolk

V The Earls of Cumberland

VI The Earls of Derby

VII The Earls of Shrewsbury

VIII The Arundells of Lanherne

IX The Seymours

X Northumberland's sons

THE LISLE PEERAGE

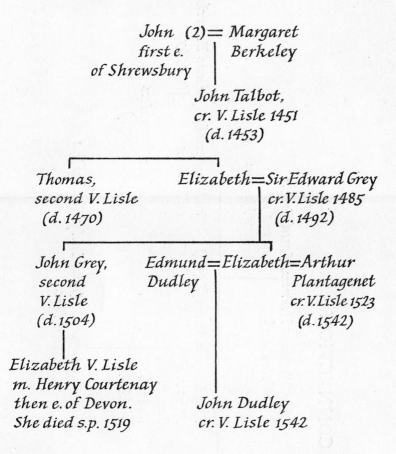

John (2)= Margaret
first e. | Berkeley
of Shrewsbury

John Talbot,
cr. V. Lisle 1451
(d. 1453)

Thomas,   Elizabeth=Sir Edward Grey
second V. Lisle   cr. V. Lisle 1485
(d. 1470)   (d. 1492)

John Grey,   Edmund=Elizabeth=Arthur
second   Dudley   Plantagenet
V. Lisle   cr. V. Lisle 1523
(d. 1504)   (d. 1542)

Elizabeth V. Lisle
m. Henry Courtenay
then e. of Devon.   John Dudley
She died s.p. 1519   cr. V. Lisle 1542

These various creations were all in right of the heirs
male of their then wife. In each case the wife had
a claim, at that date unrecognised, to the barony
of Lisle of Kingston Lisle.

THE PARR CONNECTION

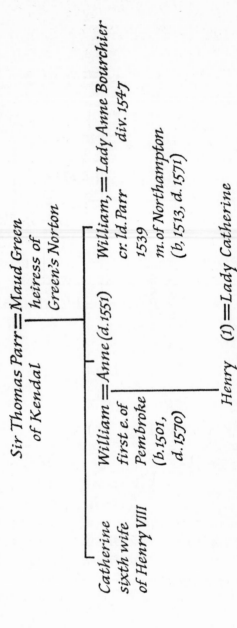

Sir Thomas Parr = Maud Green
of Kendal   heiress of
       Green's Norton

Catherine
sixth wife
of Henry VIII

William = Anne (d. 1551)
first e. of
Pembroke
(b. 1501,
d. 1570)

William, = Lady Anne Bourchier   div. 1547
cr. 1d. Parr
1539
m. of Northampton
(b, 1513, d. 1571)

Henry   (1) = Lady Catherine
1d. Herbert   Grey

THE GREY DESCENT

John Grey, = Elizabeth = Edward IV,
1d. Ferrers   Woodville   K. of England
of Groby
(d. 1461)

Thomas = Cicely, Baroness of Haryngton
first m.   and Bonville
of Dorset
(d. 1501)

Margaret = Thomas,   Lord Leonard,   Lady Elizabeth   Lady Eleanor
Wotton of   second m.   Viscount Grane   m. Gerald,   m. Sir John
Boughton   of Dorset   (d. 1541)   ninth e. of   Arundell of
Malherbe   (d. 1530)   Kildare   Lanherne

Henry, third m.   Lord Thomas   Lady Catherine   Lord John = Mary, d. of
of Dorset, later   (d. 1554)   (d. 1542)   of Pyrgo   Sir Anthony
first d. of Suffolk   m. Henry, twelfth   (d. 1569)   Browne
(d. 1554)   e. of Arundel

THE DUKES OF SUFFOLK

Mary = Charles Brandon = Katherine
Queen   first d. of Suffolk   Willoughby
of France   (d. 1545)

```
                    |                                          |
    ┌───────────────┴───────────────┐              ┌──────────┴──────────┐
 Frances =          Eleanor                       Henry              Charles
 Henry Grey,        (d. 1547)                   second d.            third d.
 m. of Dorset,      m. Henry                    of Suffolk           of Suffolk
 cr. 1551 d. of     second e. of                (d. 1551)            (d. 1551)
 Suffolk            Cumberland
 (d. 1554)              |
    |               Lady
    |               Margaret
    |               Clifford
 ┌──────────┬──────────┐
Lady       Lady       Lady
Jane       Catherine  Mary
Grey       Grey       Grey
```

THE EARLS OF CUMBERLAND

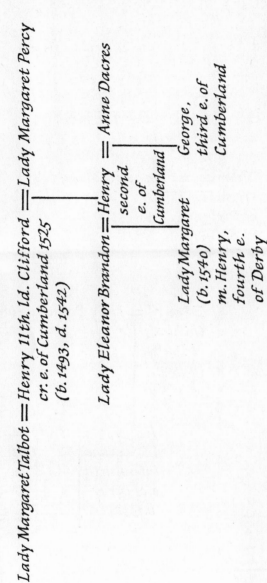

Lady Margaret Talbot = Henry 11th. ld. Clifford = Lady Margaret Percy
cr. e. of Cumberland 1525
(b. 1493, d. 1542)

Lady Eleanor Brandon = Henry = Anne Dacres
second
e. of
Cumberland

Lady Margaret
(b. 1540)
m. Henry,
fourth e.
of Derby

George,
third e. of
Cumberland

THE EARLS OF DERBY

Thomas ══ Anne Hastings
second e.
of Derby,
ld. Stanley
& Strange
(d. 1521)

Edward ══ Lady Dorothy Howard
third e.
of Derby
(b. 1509,
d. 1572)

Henry, ══ Lady Margaret
ld. Strange   Clifford
later fourth
e. of Derby
b. 1531

THE EARLS OF SHREWSBURY

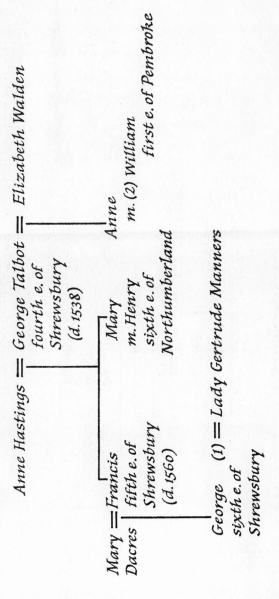

Anne Hastings = George Talbot = Elizabeth Walden
                  fourth e. of
                  Shrewsbury
                  (d. 1538)

Mary = Francis
Dacres fifth e. of
       Shrewsbury
       (d. 1560)

Mary
m. Henry
sixth e. of
Northumberland

Anne
m. (2) William
first e. of Pembroke

George   (1) = Lady Gertrude Manners
sixth e. of
Shrewsbury

M

THE ARUNDELLS OF LANHERNE

(1) Sir Thomas ══ Catherine Dynham
     Arundell of
     Lanherne

(2) Lady Elizabeth ══ Sir John ══ Jane Grenville
     Grey d. of Thomas   Arundell
     first m. of Dorset   of Lanherne

Lady Anne ══ Sir John of   Sir Thomas   Mary (d. 1557) m.·(1) Robert e. of Sussex
Stanley, d. of Lanherne   d. 1552, gr.   m. (2) Henry e. of Arundel
Edward, third   Wardour 1547 ══ Margaret Howard
e. of Derby   → sister to Queen Catherine (Howard)

(1) His younger brother Humphrey Arundell of Yewton Arundell was the
     father of Humphrey Arundell, the leader of the Western Rising.

(2) She is alternatively described as Lady Eleanor.

THE SEYMOURS

Sir John = Margaret Wentworth
Seymour of   (d. 1550)
Wolf Hall

Catherine = Edward = Anne   Jane   Thomas,
Fillol   d. of   Stanhope   third wife of   Ld. Sudeley,
           Somerset,   Henry VIII   Lord Admiral
           Lord   (d. 1549)
           Protector   m. Queen Catherine
           (b. 1506, d. 1552)   (Parr)

Edward   Edward   Anne   Jane
of Berry   e. of Hertford   m. John Dudley   (b. 1541, d. 1561)
Pomeroy   (b. 1539)   e. of Warwick

John
(d. 1551)

NORTHUMBERLAND'S SONS

John ══ Jane Guldeford
d. of
Northumberland

Sir Henry (d. 1545)	John e. of Warwick (d. 1554) m. Lady Anne Seymour	L. Ambrose, e. of Warwick (d. 1590) m. Anne Whorwood	L. Robert e. of Leicester (d. 1588) m. Amy Robsart	L. Henry (d. 1555)	L. Guildford (d. 1554) m. Lady Jane Grey

Select Bibliography

i. PRIMARY SOURCES

Calendar of State Papers, Domestic, Edward VI.
Calendar of State Papers, Venetian, ed. Rawdon Brown (1864–).
Calendar of Bath MSS at Longleat, vol. iv, Seymour Papers, 1532–1651, ed. Marjorie Blacker (1968).
Calendar of Carew MSS, vol. i.
Calendar of Sackville MSS, vol. i.i, early papers of Lionel Crabfield from 1551.
Calendar of Salisbury MSS.
A Chronicle, Henry VIII by Edward Hall, ed. C. Whibley (1904).
A Chronicle of England, vol. ii, 1547–1559 by Charles Wriothesley, Windsor Herald, ed. William Douglas-Hamilton, Camden Society (1877).
Chronicle of the Grey Friars of London, ed. J. G. Nichols, Camden Society (1852).
Chronicle and political papers of King Edward VI, ed. W. K. Jordan (1966).
Literary remains of King Edward VI, ed. J. G. Nichols, Roxburghe Club (1857).
The acts and monuments of John Foxe, ed. S. R. Catley (1841).
Works by Thomas Cranmer, ed. J. F. Cox, Parker Society (1844–6).
Works by Hugh Latimer, ed. G. F. Corrie, Parker Society (1844–5).
Seven Sermons before Edward VI by Hugh Latimer, ed. E. Arber (1869).
The Letters of Stephen Gardiner, ed. J. A. Muller (1933).

ii. SECONDARY SOURCES AND STUDIES

Lacey Baldwin Smith, *Tudor prelates and politics, 1536–1558* (1953)·
Gilbert Burnet, *The history of the reformation of the Church of England* (edition of 1865).
Hester W. Chapman, *The last Tudor king* (1958).

Hester W. Chapman, *Lady Jane Grey* (1962).

G. Constant, *The Reformation in England* (1942).

A. G. Dickens, *The English Reformation* (1964).

F. G. Emmison, *Tudor Secretary, Sir William Petre* (1961).

G. R. Elton, *The Tudor revolution in government* (1953).

James Gairdner, *The English Church in the sixteenth century* (1902).

Lady Cecily Goffe, *A woman of the Tudor Age* (1930).

Constantin Hopf, *Martin Bucer and the English Reformation* (1946).

The Rev. Philip Hughes, *The Reformation in England*, vol. ii (1954).

W. K. Jordan, *Edward VI: The Young King* (1968).

——, *Edward VI: The Threshold of Power* (1970).

Philip Lindsay, *The Queenmaker* (1951).

J. U. Nef, *Industry and government in France and England*, 1540–1640 (1940).

A. F. Pollard, *England under Protector Somerset* (1900).

F. M. Powicke, *The Reformation in England* (1941).

Jasper Ridley, *Thomas Cranmer* (1962).

Frances Rose-Troup, *The western rebellion of 1549* (1913).

A. L. Rowse, *Tudor Cornwall* (1941).

F. W. Russell, *Kett's Rebellion in Norfolk* (1859). Same title by S. T. Bindoff (1949).

T. F. Shirley, *Thomas Thirlby, Tudor Bishop* (1964).

C. H. Smyth, *Cranmer and the Reformation under Edward VI* (1926).

R. C. Strong, *Index of Jacobean Portraits* (1969).

John Strype, *The Life of Sir John Cheke* (1821).

——, *The Life and acts of Matthew Parker* (1821).

R. H. Tawney, *Religion and the rise of capitalism* (1952).

P. F. Tytler, *England under the reigns of Edward VI and Mary* (1839).

Joan Wake, *The Brudenells of Deene* (1953).

Barbara Winchester, *Tudor family portrait* (1955).

H. A. Wyndham, *The Wyndhams of Norfolk and Somerset* (1939).

Index

Abbeville, 30
Abingdon, 34
Agadir, 108
Alaska, 109
Alba, Duchess of, 164
Aldrich, Bp. Robert, 114
Aldridge, Thomas, 65
Althorp, 63
Ambleteuse, 77
Andover, 44
Angoulême, Duke of, 78
Anjou, Duke of, 78
Anne Boleyn, Queen, 28
Anne of Cleves, Queen, 25
Antwerp, 102
Archangelsk, 111
Arundel, Earl of 45, 52, 88, 139,
    145, 152
Arundell, Humphrey, 54–60
Arundell, Sir John, 54, 88
Ascham, Roger, 71
Aske, Robert, 64
Aspens, Hans, 115
Astlye, 24
Astley, Cooper, 159
Attleborough, 64
Aylmer, Dr John, 12, 71, 131
Aylmer, Hall, 131

Barbary Trade, 107
Barchampstow, 89
Barendts Sea, 110
Barking, St Mary's, 123
Barrett, Rev. Roger, 58
Basing House, 135
Basingstoke, 44

Bassett, Katharine, 35
Bath, Earl of, 39
Bath and Wells, see of, 114
Bavaria, Philip of, 34
Bavaria, Princesses of,
    Sabina, 128
    Sibylla, 128
    Sidonia, 128
    Susanna, 128
Beaudesert, 87
Beaujeu, Anne, 41
Beaulieu, 44, 135
Bedford, Earl of, 83, 97, 147
    Countess of, 97
Bekinshaw, John, 30
Benin, Coast of, 108
Bering Straits, 109
Bering, Vitus, 109
Biche, 102
Bodmin, 56, 57
Body, Rev. William, 57
Bonner, Bp. Edmund, 114
Boulogne, 38, 61
Bourburg Abbey, 33
Bourchier, Lord, 32
    Lady Anne, 83
Bradgate Park, 11, 34
Bramber, Rape of, 20
Bramshott, 20
Brandenburg, Elector of, 128
Brandon see Suffolk
Breda, 102
Brest, 24
Bristol, 109
    Mint at, 74
Bristol Venturers, 110

Browne, Sir Anthony, 43
Browne, Sir William, 123
Brussels, 102–3
Palais de Nassau, 102
Buckden, 133
Buckenham, 24
Buckingham, Duke of, 27
Bullinger, Johann Heinrich, 132
Burghley House, 91
Burton Constable, 114
Bury St Edmunds, 149
Bush, Bp. Paul, 114
Buttall, Sir Gregory, 33

Cabot, Sebastian, 109
Calais
    Castle, 32–5
        Basse Cour of, 30
    Castle Hill, 31
    Boulogne Gate at, 31
    Dunkirk Gate at, 31
    Lantern Gate at, 31, 35
    Milk Gate at, 31
    Water Gate at, 31
    Carmelite House at, 33
    Market of the Staple at, 31
    Rose, Inn at, 33
Calais Roads, 35
Calbourne, 20
Calvinism, 49, 73, 99, 127
Cambridge, 67, 79, 150–1
    King's College, 144
    Market Cross, 144
    Market, Place, 151
    Queens' College, 71
    St John's College, 89
    St Mary's Church, 78
    Trinity College, 78
Castle Hedingham, 148
Castle Rising, 65
Catcombe, 20

Catherine of Aragon, Queen, 27, 105
Catherine II, Tsarina, 110
Cathay Passage to, 109
Chamberlayne, Sir Leonard, 93
Chancellor, Richard, 110–11
Charles V, Emperor, 101–3
Charles VIII of France, King, 41
Charnwood Forest, 11
Chateaubriant, 79
Chatillon, 23
Cheke, Sir John, 76, 89–91
Cheshunt, 72
Clifford see Cumberland
    Lady Margaret, 126
Clinton, Lord, 39, 90
Clouet, François, 101
Cobham, Lord, 83
Codd, Thomas, 65
Colet, Dean, 21
Coligny, Gaspard de, 73
Compton, Peter, 137
Compton Winyates, 137
Condé, Princess of, 129
Constantine, 57
Cooke, Sir Anthony, 76, 89
Coughton, 94
Courtenay, Lord, 41
Coverdale, Bp. Miles, 57
Cowdray, 135
Cranmer, Abp. Thomas, 15–16, 80, 117, 145, 161
Crediton, 59
Crewkerne, 57
Cromwell, Thomas, 115
Cumberland, Earl of, 93, 97
    Countess of, 126

Dacre, Lord, 57, 95–7
Darcy, Lord, 145

Day, Bp. George, 114
Dee, John, 110
Denny, Sir Anthony, 43–4, 72
Derby, Earl of, 51, 92–3, 139
Devon, Countess of, 24–5
Doria, Andrea, 79
Dormer, Sir William, 94
Dorset, Marquess of, 12, 34, 51, 73, 131
  Marchioness of, 34, 126, 130–1
Dorset see also Suffolk
Drake, Sir Francis, 99
Drayton, 149
Dudley see Northumberland
Dudley Castle, 21
Dudley, Lords, 21
  Edmund 9–21
  Lord Ambrose, 69, 147, 148
  Lord Guildford, 69, 143–60 passim
  Lord Henry, 69
  Lord John, 84, 148
  Lord Robert, 53, 69, 127, 148
Dunkirk, 31
Dunster, 107
Dussin's Dale, 67

East Friesland, Countess of, 119
Eden, Richard, 107
Edward IV, King, 24
Edward VI, King, 44–88, 126–41 passim
Elizabeth, Lady, 41, 70–2, 76, 127
Elmina, 108
Ely, Isle of, 151
Emden, 119
Empson, Sir Richard, 19–21
Essex see Northampton
Etampes, Duchess of, 30
Ethiopia, Emperor of, 107
Ewyas, 137

Exe Island, 58
Exeter, 59
  Marchioness of, 87

Feria, Duchess of, 94
Ferrar, Bp. Robert, 161
Ferrara, Duchess of, 129
Fez, Kingdom of, 107
Fillol, Sir William, 38
Fisher, Bp. John, 27
FitzAlan see Arundel
FitzAlan, Lady Catherine, 46
FitzJames, Bp. Richard, 21
Fitzpatrick, Barnaby, 14, 76, 135
Flicke, Gerlach, 81
Flodden, battle of, 24
Florida, 106
Foxe, Edward, 63
Framlingham, 112, 143–6, 148
Frisius, Gemma, 110
Frobisher, Martin, 108
Fulford, Sir John, 54

Gardiner, Bp. Stephen, 36, 56, 74, 88, 148
Garrard, Sir William, 108
Gassel, Lucas van, 102
Gates, Sir John, 156
Gidea Park, 88
Gilbert, Sir Humphrey, 99
Gilsland, 96
Gold Coast, 108
Gonson, William, 40
Goodrich, Bp. Thomas, 145, 156
Gravelines, 33
  Crown Inn at, 33
Great Fulford, 54
Greatworth Manor, 114
Greenland, 109
Grey see Dorset, Suffolk

Grey, Lady Jane, 12 and 130–60
    passim.
  birth and descent, 12
  education, 72–3
  upbringing, 130–2
  approach to
  religion, 132–3
  marriage, 138
  marital life, 143
  reign, 139–50
Grey, Lady Catherine, 136, 138,
    156, 160
  Lady Mary, 138, 155, 159
  Lord John, 159
Grey de Wilton, Lord, 159
Greystoke, barony, 97
Grindal, William, 71
Guilford, Sir Edward, 25
Guise, Duke of, 77

Hackforth, 115
Haddington, 61
Hakluyt, Richard, 107
Halesowen, 164
Hallingbury Morley, 94
Halnaker, 135
Hampton Court, 51, 64
Hampton Park Chase, 57
Hanseatic League, 111
Hastings, Sir Edward, 148
Havant, 135
Hawkins, Sir John, 99
Heath, Bp. Nicholas, 114
Holland, 54
Hengrave Hall, 144
Henry VII, King, 19, 20
Henry VIII, King, 11–54 *passim*
Henry III of France, King, 15, 75,
    101
Henry II of France, King, 78
Herbert *see* Pembroke

Herbert, Sir Richard, 137
Hesse, Philip of, 128
Hilliard, Nicholas, 49
Hinton, St George, 39
Hoddesdon, 143
Hoghton, Thomas, 92
Hoghton Tower, 93
Holt Castle, 74
Holyman, Bp. John 94
Hooper, Bp. John, 119, 161
Hopton, Dr John, 87
Hot Gospeller *see* Underhill
Howard *see* Norfolk, Surrey
    Queen Catherine, 36
Howard of Effingham, Lord, 39
Hudson Strait, 109
Hungary, Queen of, 102
Huntingdon, Earl of, 98, 99, 155
    Countess of, 98

Ilminster, 39
Ingatestone Hall, 123–5
Ivan IV, Tsar, 111

Jerningham, Sir Richard, 97
Jouarre, Abbess of, 129

Kendal, 57
Kenilworth, 24
    Constable of, 24, 34
Kenninghall, 86, 143
Kett, Robert 64–8
    William, 64, 68
Kilter, William, 57
King's Lynn, 151
Kingston Lisle, 13, 22–6
Kirby Wiske, 71
Kitchin, Bp. Anthony, 114
Knox, John, 120
Knyvett, Sir Thomas, 24

Labrador, 109
Lambert, Francis, 108
Lanercost, 95
Lanherne, 54
Lasco, John à, 119
Latimer, Bp. Hugh, 70, 152, 161
Laud, Abp. William, 132
Laval de Boisdauphin, René de
   103
Lees Priory, 49
Le Havre, 151
Leicester, Earl of, 53
Leith, 61
Le Métail, Guillaume, 30
Lennox, Countess of, 127
Lewes, priory at, 45
L'Hôpital, Michel de, 120
Lichfield, diocese of, 92
Liddington, 89
London,
  Aldersgate, 124
  Baynard's Castle, 145, 150
  Bloomsbury, 44
  Cannon Row, 89
  Chelsea, 139
  Chelsea Manor, 164
  Coldharbour, 116
  Dorset Place, 134
  Drapers' Company, 123
  Durham House, 140
  Ely House, 83
  Gray's Inn, 20
  Lambeth, 118
  Little Britain, 123
  Long Lane, 123
  Paul's Wharf, 123
  St Swithin's Lane, 20
  Southampton House, 44
  Strand, the, 124
  Suffolk House, 137
  Swan Inn, 123

Thames Street, 116
Whitefriars, 117
London, Tower of, 35, 83
  Armoury of, 28
  Bayward Tower, 153
  Beauchamp Tower, 153
  Bell Tower, 154
  Curfew Tower, 153
  Garden Tower, 153
  Great Hall, 145
  Jewel House, 147
  Lion Gate, 153
  Lion Tower, 153
  Mr Partridge's house, 157
  Royal Landing Stage, 140
  State Rooms, 142
  White Tower, 153, 161
London Churches,
  All Hallows, Bread Street, 120
  Austin Friars, 119
  St Agnes and St Anne, 87
  St Anthony, Threadneedle
    Street, 119
  St Bartholomew's Priory, 123
  St Botolph-without-Aldersgate,
    124
  St Paul's, 21
  Westminster Abbey, 21, 51-2
Longleat, 49, 50
Louis XI, of France, King, 19
Lumley, Lord, 45, 76
Luttrell, Sir John, 108

Macedonia, Prince of, 79
Maitland of Leathington, 121
Mallett, Rev. Francis, 87
Maltravers, Lord, 51, 76
Marguerite of Navarre, 71
Mariemont, 102
Mary, Lady, 41, 87, 126, 140-1,
  145

Matochkin Shar, 110
Mauritania, 107
Mayenne, Marquis de, 47
Mecklenburg, Duke of, 79
Mehedia, 79
Mendoza, Diego de, 164
Mercator, Gerard, 110
Micheldever, 44
Milan, 101
Montagu, Viscount, 97,
Montague, Sir Edward, 138
Montmorency, Constable de, 102
Montpensier, Duke of, 79
Mordaunt, Lord, 94
    Sir John, 94
More, Sir Thomas, 27, 115
Morley, Lord, 57, 94
Moryson, Sir Richard, 132
Moscow, 111, 112
Mount Surrey, 63
Mousehold Heath, 65-7

Naples, 33, 101
Navarre, Queen of, 131
Nettlestead, 27
Newdigate, Sebastian, 93
Newfoundland, 109
Newhall, 86
Noailles, Antoine de, 103
Norfolk, Duke of, 36, 62-3, 144,
    154
Northallerton, 71
Northampton, Marquess of, 42,
    66-7, 83, 154
North-East Passage, 109
North-West Passage, 109
Northumberland, Duke of,
    birth and descent, 22-4
    training at court, 27-9
    preparing for power, 39-53
    the years of power, 85-154

Northumberland, Duchess of, 98,
    106, 142-3, 160, 164-5
Novaya Zemlya, 110-11
Novgorod, 111

Orange, Prince of, 102
Ostrich, Henry, 108
Oxford,
    All Souls College, 122
    Blackfriars, 87
Oxford, Earl of, 50, 148

Padua, 115
Paget, Sir William, 49, 50, 83
Palatine, Electors,
    Louis V, 128
    Otto Henry, 128
Palmer, Sir Thomas, 156
Paris, 30
Parker, Sir Henry, 54
    Dr Matthew, 78
Parma, 79
Parr, see Northampton,
    Queen Catherine, 17, 37, 50,
    70-2
Parris, George van, 78
Paul IV, Pope, 162
Paulet, Amyas, 59
    Sir Hugh, 59
Paulet see Winchester
Peckham, Sir Edmund, 44
Pembroke, Earl of, 42, 53, 136-7
Penshurst, 166
Périgord, 23
Petre, Sir William, 91, 121, 122-5
Petworth, 135
PfalzGraf see Bavaria, Philip of
Philip II of Spain, 161
Plantagenet, Arthur, 25, 30-5
Pole, Reginald Cardinal, 33, 41
Portsmouth, 135

Portugal, Prince of, 79
Pyrton, 95

Radcliffe *see* Sussex
Rampton, 38
Reading, 135
Reigate, 63
Renaud, Simon, 105
Ribblesdale, 92
Richmond, Duke of, 39
  Duchess of, 63
Rich, Lord, 49
Ridley, Bp. Nicholas, 76, 119, 152, 161
Riga, 111
Robsart, Sir John, 69
Rolvenden, 25
Rosenberg, House of, 106
Rouen, 79,
Rudolf II, Emperor, 106
Rugg, Bp. William, 65, 114
Russell, Lord, 31, 45
Rutland, Countess of, 33

Sadler, Sir Ralph, 44
St André, Maréchal de, 77
St Benet's, Hulme, 65
St John *see* Winchester
St Keverne, 87
St Michael's Mount, 54
Salisbury, 135
Samlesbury, 92
Sampford Courtenay, 57, 59
Sandys, Dr Edwin, 149
Savernake Forest, 14, 73
Saveuses, Madame de, 31
Sawston, 143
Scheyfve, Jean, 103
Schlettstadt, 78
Scilly Islands, 74
Scrope of Bolton, Lord, 71

Sharington, Sir William, 74
Sheen, 16, 145
Sheffield Castle, 96
Seymour *see* Somerset,
  Queen Jane, 40
Seymour of Sudeley, Lord, 40, 47, 50, 69–74
Sheen, 16, 145
Ships,
  Ark Royal, 39
  Bona Esperanza, 111
  Bonaventure Edward, 111
  Confidentia, 111
  Henry Grace à Dieu, 39
  Lion, 107–8
  Moon, 108
  Primrose, 108
  Squirrel, 99
Shirburn Castle, 93
Shrewsbury, Earl of, 51, 57, 94–6, 145
Siberia, 109
Siderstern, 69
Sidney, Sir Henry, 165
  Lady Mary, 139, 164
Somerset, Duke of,
  birth and descent, 37
  character, 13–14, 37
  Protectorate of, 49–83
Somerset, Duchess of, 38, 87, 149
Somersham, 156
Southampton, Earl of, 44–5
Southwell, Sir Robert, 62
Southworth, Sir John, 92
Stamford St Martin, 91
Stanwell, 25
Stokes, Adrian, 160
Stonor, Cecily, Lady, 93
  Sir Francis, 93
Stourton, Lord, 25, 116–17

Stow, 132
Sudeley Castle, 72
Suffolk, Dukes of (Brandons), 28,
    41, 48, 133
Suffolk, Duke of (*see* Dorset), 133,
    142–61
    Duchess of, 134, 142–56, 160
Surrey, Earl of, 36–8
Sussex, Earl of, 144
Syon, 129, 145
Sutton Coldfield, 55

Tavistock, 57
Tehidy, 30
Thérouanne, 31
Thetford, 67, 89
Thomassin, 74
Thompson, Rev. John, 58
Thorndon Hall, 122
Throckmorton, Sir Clement, 94
    Sir George, 94
    Sir Nicholas, 94
Thurland Castle, 97, 115
Titchfield, 44
Tivetshall St Mary, 131
Torbryan, 122
Torrington, 57
Toul, diocese of, 101
Towcester, 20
Tregarrick, 57
Trevian, Pascoe, 57
Tunstall, Bp. Cuthbert, 113–17
Turvey, 94
Tyrrell, Sir John, 123

Ugrian Strait, 110
Ulmis, John de, 132
Underhill, Edward, 75

Vane, Sir Ralph, 88

Vardohuus, 111
Vaux, Lord, 139
Verdun, diocese of, 101
Veysey, Bp. John, 55–6
Vesoul, 103
Vyvyan, Bp. John, 56

Wallenstein, Wenzel Eusebius von,
    106
Walsingham, Our Lady of, 26
Wardour Castle, 54
Warley, 123
Warwick, dukedom of, 53
Westmoreland, Earl of, 138
Wharton, Lord, 57
    Lady, 96
White Horse, Vale of the, 24
Whitehead, James, 116
Willoughby, Sir Edward, 135
    Sir Hugh, 111
    Sir John, 26
Wilton Abbey, 42
Wimbledon, 89
Winchester, 44
Winchester, Marquess of, 16, 49,
    85, 145, 146–7
Windsor Castle, 23, 135
Windsor, Lord, 57, 148
Wing, 94
Wingfield, Sir Anthony, 71
Winslade, John, 57, 60
Winwood, William, 69
Wittlesea Mere, 89
Wolaton, 26, 111
Wolsey, Thomas Cardinal, 115
Wootton Basset, 34
Worcester, Earl of, 138
Wroth, Sir Thomas, 108
Wyatt, Sir Thomas, 161
Wymondham, 70
Wyndham, Thomas, 107

Yarmouth, 65
York, 93
Yorke, Sir John, 108

Zafia, 108
Zurich, 119
Zwingli, Hildreich, 127